Mometrix TEST PREPARATION

TExES

Educational Diagnostician (253) Secrets Study Guide

I0878851

DEAR FUTURE EXAM SUCCESS STORY

First of all, **THANK YOU** for purchasing Mometrix study materials!

Second, congratulations! You are one of the few determined test-takers who are committed to doing whatever it takes to excel on your exam. **You have come to the right place.** We developed these study materials with one goal in mind: to deliver you the information you need in a format that's concise and easy to use.

In addition to optimizing your guide for the content of the test, we've outlined our recommended steps for breaking down the preparation process into small, attainable goals so you can make sure you stay on track.

We've also analyzed the entire test-taking process, identifying the most common pitfalls and showing how you can overcome them and be ready for any curveball the test throws you.

Standardized testing is one of the biggest obstacles on your road to success, which only increases the importance of doing well in the high-pressure, high-stakes environment of test day. Your results on this test could have a significant impact on your future, and this guide provides the information and practical advice to help you achieve your full potential on test day.

Your success is our success

We would love to hear from you! If you would like to share the story of your exam success or if you have any questions or comments in regard to our products, please contact us at **800-673-8175** or **support@mometrix.com**.

Thanks again for your business and we wish you continued success!

Sincerely,
The Mometrix Test Preparation Team

Need more help? Check out our flashcards at:
http://mometrixflashcards.com/TExES

Copyright © 2026 by Mometrix Media LLC. All rights reserved.
Written and edited by the Mometrix Exam Secrets Test Prep Team
Printed in the United States of America

TABLE OF CONTENTS

Introduction

Thank you for purchasing this resource! You have made the choice to prepare yourself for a test that could have a huge impact on your future, and this guide is designed to help you be fully ready for test day. Obviously, it's important to have a solid understanding of the test material, but you also need to be prepared for the unique environment and stressors of the test, so that you can perform to the best of your abilities.

For this purpose, the first section that appears in this guide is the **Secret Keys**. We've devoted countless hours to meticulously researching what works and what doesn't, and we've boiled down our findings to the five most impactful steps you can take to improve your performance on the test. We start at the beginning with study planning and move through the preparation process, all the way to the testing strategies that will help you get the most out of what you know when you're finally sitting in front of the test.

We recommend that you start preparing for your test as far in advance as possible. However, if you've bought this guide as a last-minute study resource and only have a few days before your test, we recommend that you skip over the first two Secret Keys since they address a long-term study plan.

If you struggle with **test anxiety**, we strongly encourage you to check out our recommendations for how you can overcome it. Test anxiety is a formidable foe, but it can be beaten, and we want to make sure you have the tools you need to defeat it.

Copyright © Mometrix Media. You have been licensed one copy of this document for personal use only. Any other reproduction or redistribution is strictly prohibited. All rights reserved.
This content is provided for test preparation purposes only and does not imply an endorsement by Mometrix of any particular political, scientific, or religious point of view.

Secret Key #1 – Plan Big, Study Small

There's a lot riding on your performance. If you want to ace this test, you're going to need to keep your skills sharp and the material fresh in your mind. You need a plan that lets you review everything you need to know while still fitting in your schedule. We'll break this strategy down into three categories.

Information Organization

Start with the information you already have: the official test outline. From this, you can make a complete list of all the concepts you need to cover before the test. Organize these concepts into groups that can be studied together, and create a list of any related vocabulary you need to learn so you can brush up on any difficult terms. You'll want to keep this vocabulary list handy once you actually start studying since you may need to add to it along the way.

Time Management

Once you have your set of study concepts, decide how to spread them out over the time you have left before the test. Break your study plan into small, clear goals so you have a manageable task for each day and know exactly what you're doing. Then just focus on one small step at a time. When you manage your time this way, you don't need to spend hours at a time studying. Studying a small block of content for a short period each day helps you retain information better and avoid stressing over how much you have left to do. You can relax knowing that you have a plan to cover everything in time. In order for this strategy to be effective though, you have to start studying early and stick to your schedule. Avoid the exhaustion and futility that comes from last-minute cramming!

Study Environment

The environment you study in has a big impact on your learning. Studying in a coffee shop, while probably more enjoyable, is not likely to be as fruitful as studying in a quiet room. It's important to keep distractions to a minimum. You're only planning to study for a short block of time, so make the most of it. Don't pause to check your phone or get up to find a snack. It's also important to **avoid multitasking**. Research has consistently shown that multitasking will make your studying dramatically less effective. Your study area should also be comfortable and well-lit so you don't have the distraction of straining your eyes or sitting on an uncomfortable chair.

The time of day you study is also important. You want to be rested and alert. Don't wait until just before bedtime. Study when you'll be most likely to comprehend and remember. Even better, if you know what time of day your test will be, set that time aside for study. That way your brain will be used to working on that subject at that specific time and you'll have a better chance of recalling information.

Finally, it can be helpful to team up with others who are studying for the same test. Your actual studying should be done in as isolated an environment as possible, but the work of organizing the information and setting up the study plan can be divided up. In between study sessions, you can discuss with your teammates the concepts that you're all studying and quiz each other on the details. Just be sure that your teammates are as serious about the test as you are. If you find that your study time is being replaced with social time, you might need to find a new team.

Copyright © Mometrix Media. You have been licensed one copy of this document for personal use only. Any other reproduction or redistribution is strictly prohibited. All rights reserved.
This content is provided for test preparation purposes only and does not imply an endorsement by Mometrix of any particular political, scientific, or religious point of view.

Secret Key #2 – Make Your Studying Count

You're devoting a lot of time and effort to preparing for this test, so you want to be absolutely certain it will pay off. This means doing more than just reading the content and hoping you can remember it on test day. It's important to make every minute of study count. There are two main areas you can focus on to make your studying count.

Retention

It doesn't matter how much time you study if you can't remember the material. You need to make sure you are retaining the concepts. To check your retention of the information you're learning, try recalling it at later times with minimal prompting. Try carrying around flashcards and glance at one or two from time to time or ask a friend who's also studying for the test to quiz you.

To enhance your retention, look for ways to put the information into practice so that you can apply it rather than simply recalling it. If you're using the information in practical ways, it will be much easier to remember. Similarly, it helps to solidify a concept in your mind if you're not only reading it to yourself but also explaining it to someone else. Ask a friend to let you teach them about a concept you're a little shaky on (or speak aloud to an imaginary audience if necessary). As you try to summarize, define, give examples, and answer your friend's questions, you'll understand the concepts better and they will stay with you longer. Finally, step back for a big picture view and ask yourself how each piece of information fits with the whole subject. When you link the different concepts together and see them working together as a whole, it's easier to remember the individual components.

Finally, practice showing your work on any multi-step problems, even if you're just studying. Writing out each step you take to solve a problem will help solidify the process in your mind, and you'll be more likely to remember it during the test.

Modality

Modality simply refers to the means or method by which you study. Choosing a study modality that fits your own individual learning style is crucial. No two people learn best in exactly the same way, so it's important to know your strengths and use them to your advantage.

For example, if you learn best by visualization, focus on visualizing a concept in your mind and draw an image or a diagram. Try color-coding your notes, illustrating them, or creating symbols that will trigger your mind to recall a learned concept. If you learn best by hearing or discussing information, find a study partner who learns the same way or read aloud to yourself. Think about how to put the information in your own words. Imagine that you are giving a lecture on the topic and record yourself so you can listen to it later.

For any learning style, flashcards can be helpful. Organize the information so you can take advantage of spare moments to review. Underline key words or phrases. Use different colors for different categories. Mnemonic devices (such as creating a short list in which every item starts with the same letter) can also help with retention. Find what works best for you and use it to store the information in your mind most effectively and easily.

Copyright © Mometrix Media. You have been licensed one copy of this document for personal use only. Any other reproduction or redistribution is strictly prohibited. All rights reserved.
This content is provided for test preparation purposes only and does not imply an endorsement by Mometrix of any particular political, scientific, or religious point of view.

Secret Key #3 – Practice the Right Way

Your success on test day depends not only on how many hours you put into preparing, but also on whether you prepared the right way. It's good to check along the way to see if your studying is paying off. One of the most effective ways to do this is by taking practice tests to evaluate your progress. Practice tests are useful because they show exactly where you need to improve. Every time you take a practice test, pay special attention to these three groups of questions:

- The questions you got wrong
- The questions you had to guess on, even if you guessed right
- The questions you found difficult or slow to work through

This will show you exactly what your weak areas are, and where you need to devote more study time. Ask yourself why each of these questions gave you trouble. Was it because you didn't understand the material? Was it because you didn't remember the vocabulary? Do you need more repetitions on this type of question to build speed and confidence? Dig into those questions and figure out how you can strengthen your weak areas as you go back to review the material.

Additionally, many practice tests have a section explaining the answer choices. It can be tempting to read the explanation and think that you now have a good understanding of the concept. However, an explanation likely only covers part of the question's broader context. Even if the explanation makes perfect sense, **go back and investigate** every concept related to the question until you're positive you have a thorough understanding.

As you go along, keep in mind that the practice test is just that: practice. Memorizing these questions and answers will not be very helpful on the actual test because it is unlikely to have any of the same exact questions. If you only know the right answers to the sample questions, you won't be prepared for the real thing. **Study the concepts** until you understand them fully, and then you'll be able to answer any question that shows up on the test.

It's important to wait on the practice tests until you're ready. If you take a test on your first day of study, you may be overwhelmed by the amount of material covered and how much you need to learn. Work up to it gradually.

On test day, you'll need to be prepared for answering questions, managing your time, and using the test-taking strategies you've learned. It's a lot to balance, like a mental marathon that will have a big impact on your future. Like training for a marathon, you'll need to start slowly and work your way up. When test day arrives, you'll be ready.

Start with the strategies you've read in the first two Secret Keys—plan your course and study in the way that works best for you. If you have time, consider using multiple study resources to get different approaches to the same concepts. It can be helpful to see difficult concepts from more than one angle. Then find a good source for practice tests. Many times, the test website will suggest potential study resources or provide sample tests.

Copyright © Mometrix Media. You have been licensed one copy of this document for personal use only. Any other reproduction or redistribution is strictly prohibited. All rights reserved.
This content is provided for test preparation purposes only and does not imply an endorsement by Mometrix of any particular political, scientific, or religious point of view.

Practice Test Strategy

If you're able to find at least three practice tests, we recommend this strategy:

Untimed and Open-Book Practice

Take the first test with no time constraints and with your notes and study guide handy. Take your time and focus on applying the strategies you've learned.

Timed and Open-Book Practice

Take the second practice test open-book as well, but set a timer and practice pacing yourself to finish in time.

Timed and Closed-Book Practice

Take any other practice tests as if it were test day. Set a timer and put away your study materials. Sit at a table or desk in a quiet room, imagine yourself at the testing center, and answer questions as quickly and accurately as possible.

Keep repeating timed and closed-book tests on a regular basis until you run out of practice tests or it's time for the actual test. Your mind will be ready for the schedule and stress of test day, and you'll be able to focus on recalling the material you've learned.

Copyright © Mometrix Media. You have been licensed one copy of this document for personal use only. Any other reproduction or redistribution is strictly prohibited. All rights reserved.
This content is provided for test preparation purposes only and does not imply an endorsement by Mometrix of any particular political, scientific, or religious point of view.

Secret Key #4 – Pace Yourself

Once you're fully prepared for the material on the test, your biggest challenge on test day will be managing your time. Just knowing that the clock is ticking can make you panic even if you have plenty of time left. Work on pacing yourself so you can build confidence against the time constraints of the exam. Pacing is a difficult skill to master, especially in a high-pressure environment, so **practice is vital**.

Set time expectations for your pace based on how much time is available. For example, if a section has 60 questions and the time limit is 30 minutes, you know you have to average 30 seconds or less per question in order to answer them all. Although 30 seconds is the hard limit, set 25 seconds per question as your goal, so you reserve extra time to spend on harder questions. When you budget extra time for the harder questions, you no longer have any reason to stress when those questions take longer to answer.

Don't let this time expectation distract you from working through the test at a calm, steady pace, but keep it in mind so you don't spend too much time on any one question. Recognize that taking extra time on one question you don't understand may keep you from answering two that you do understand later in the test. If your time limit for a question is up and you're still not sure of the answer, mark it and move on, and come back to it later if the time and the test format allow. If the testing format doesn't allow you to return to earlier questions, just make an educated guess; then put it out of your mind and move on.

On the easier questions, be careful not to rush. It may seem wise to hurry through them so you have more time for the challenging ones, but it's not worth missing one if you know the concept and just didn't take the time to read the question fully. Work efficiently but make sure you understand the question and have looked at all of the answer choices, since more than one may seem right at first.

Even if you're paying attention to the time, you may find yourself a little behind at some point. You should speed up to get back on track, but do so wisely. Don't panic; just take a few seconds less on each question until you're caught up. Don't guess without thinking, but do look through the answer choices and eliminate any you know are wrong. If you can get down to two choices, it is often worthwhile to guess from those. Once you've chosen an answer, move on and don't dwell on any that you skipped or had to hurry through. If a question was taking too long, chances are it was one of the harder ones, so you weren't as likely to get it right anyway.

On the other hand, if you find yourself getting ahead of schedule, it may be beneficial to slow down a little. The more quickly you work, the more likely you are to make a careless mistake that will affect your score. You've budgeted time for each question, so don't be afraid to spend that time. Practice an efficient but careful pace to get the most out of the time you have.

Copyright © Mometrix Media. You have been licensed one copy of this document for personal use only. Any other reproduction or redistribution is strictly prohibited. All rights reserved.
This content is provided for test preparation purposes only and does not imply an endorsement by Mometrix of any particular political, scientific, or religious point of view.

Secret Key #5 – Have a Plan for Guessing

When you're taking the test, you may find yourself stuck on a question. Some of the answer choices seem better than others, but you don't see the one answer choice that is obviously correct. What do you do?

The scenario described above is very common, yet most test takers have not effectively prepared for it. Developing and practicing a plan for guessing may be one of the single most effective uses of your time as you get ready for the exam.

In developing your plan for guessing, there are three questions to address:

- When should you start the guessing process?
- How should you narrow down the choices?
- Which answer should you choose?

When to Start the Guessing Process

Unless your plan for guessing is to select C every time (which, despite its merits, is not what we recommend), you need to leave yourself enough time to apply your answer elimination strategies. Since you have a limited amount of time for each question, that means that if you're going to give yourself the best shot at guessing correctly, you have to decide quickly whether or not you will guess.

Of course, the best-case scenario is that you don't have to guess at all, so first, see if you can answer the question based on your knowledge of the subject and basic reasoning skills. Focus on the key words in the question and try to jog your memory of related topics. Give yourself a chance to bring the knowledge to mind, but once you realize that you don't have (or you can't access) the knowledge you need to answer the question, it's time to start the guessing process.

It's almost always better to start the guessing process too early than too late. It only takes a few seconds to remember something and answer the question from knowledge. Carefully eliminating wrong answer choices takes longer. Plus, going through the process of eliminating answer choices can actually help jog your memory.

Summary: Start the guessing process as soon as you decide that you can't answer the question based on your knowledge.

Copyright © Mometrix Media. You have been licensed one copy of this document for personal use only. Any other reproduction or redistribution is strictly prohibited. All rights reserved.
This content is provided for test preparation purposes only and does not imply an endorsement by Mometrix of any particular political, scientific, or religious point of view.

How to Narrow Down the Choices

The next chapter in this book (**Test-Taking Strategies**) includes a wide range of strategies for how to approach questions and how to look for answer choices to eliminate. You will definitely want to read those carefully, practice them, and figure out which ones work best for you. Here though, we're going to address a mindset rather than a particular strategy.

Your odds of guessing an answer correctly depend on how many options you are choosing from.

Number of options left	5	4	3	2	1
Odds of guessing correctly	20%	25%	33%	50%	100%

You can see from this chart just how valuable it is to be able to eliminate incorrect answers and make an educated guess, but there are two things that many test takers do that cause them to miss out on the benefits of guessing:

- Accidentally eliminating the correct answer
- Selecting an answer based on an impression

We'll look at the first one here, and the second one in the next section.

To avoid accidentally eliminating the correct answer, we recommend a thought exercise called **the $5 challenge**. In this challenge, you only eliminate an answer choice from contention if you are willing to bet $5 on it being wrong. Why $5? Five dollars is a small but not insignificant amount of money. It's an amount you could afford to lose but wouldn't want to throw away. And while losing $5 once might not hurt too much, doing it twenty times will set you back $100. In the same way, each small decision you make—eliminating a choice here, guessing on a question there—won't by itself impact your score very much, but when you put them all together, they can make a big difference. By holding each answer choice elimination decision to a higher standard, you can reduce the risk of accidentally eliminating the correct answer.

The $5 challenge can also be applied in a positive sense: If you are willing to bet $5 that an answer choice *is* correct, go ahead and mark it as correct.

Summary: Only eliminate an answer choice if you are willing to bet $5 that it is wrong.

Copyright © Mometrix Media. You have been licensed one copy of this document for personal use only. Any other reproduction or redistribution is strictly prohibited. All rights reserved.
This content is provided for test preparation purposes only and does not imply an endorsement by Mometrix of any particular political, scientific, or religious point of view.

Which Answer to Choose

You're taking the test. You've run into a hard question and decided you'll have to guess. You've eliminated all the answer choices you're willing to bet $5 on. Now you have to pick an answer. Why do we even need to talk about this? Why can't you just pick whichever one you feel like when the time comes?

The answer to these questions is that if you don't come into the test with a plan, you'll rely on your impression to select an answer choice, and if you do that, you risk falling into a trap. The test writers know that everyone who takes their test will be guessing on some of the questions, so they intentionally write wrong answer choices to seem plausible. You still have to pick an answer though, and if the wrong answer choices are designed to look right, how can you ever be sure that you're not falling for their trap? The best solution we've found to this dilemma is to take the decision out of your hands entirely. Here is the process we recommend:

Once you've eliminated any choices that you are confident (willing to bet $5) are wrong, select the first remaining choice as your answer.

Whether you choose to select the first remaining choice, the second, or the last, the important thing is that you use some preselected standard. Using this approach guarantees that you will not be enticed into selecting an answer choice that looks right, because you are not basing your decision on how the answer choices look.

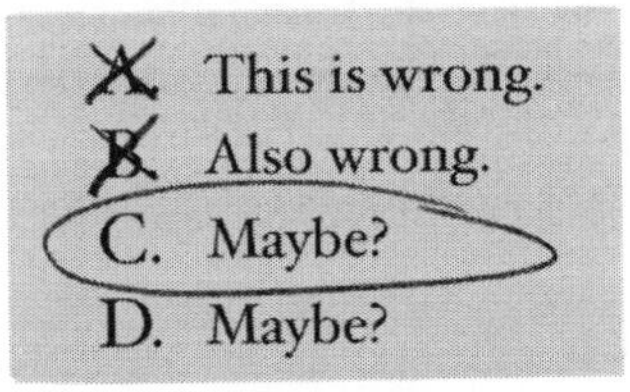

This is not meant to make you question your knowledge. Instead, it is to help you recognize the difference between your knowledge and your impressions. There's a huge difference between thinking an answer is right because of what you know, and thinking an answer is right because it looks or sounds like it should be right.

Summary: To ensure that your selection is appropriately random, make a predetermined selection from among all answer choices you have not eliminated.

Copyright © Mometrix Media. You have been licensed one copy of this document for personal use only. Any other reproduction or redistribution is strictly prohibited. All rights reserved.
This content is provided for test preparation purposes only and does not imply an endorsement by Mometrix of any particular political, scientific, or religious point of view.

Test-Taking Strategies

This section contains a list of test-taking strategies that you may find helpful as you work through the test. By taking what you know and applying logical thought, you can maximize your chances of answering any question correctly!

It is very important to realize that every question is different and every person is different: no single strategy will work on every question, and no single strategy will work for every person. That's why we've included all of them here, so you can try them out and determine which ones work best for different types of questions and which ones work best for you.

Question Strategies

✓ Read Carefully

Read the question and the answer choices carefully. Don't miss the question because you misread the terms. You have plenty of time to read each question thoroughly and make sure you understand what is being asked. Yet a happy medium must be attained, so don't waste too much time. You must read carefully and efficiently.

✓ Contextual Clues

Look for contextual clues. If the question includes a word you are not familiar with, look at the immediate context for some indication of what the word might mean. Contextual clues can often give you all the information you need to decipher the meaning of an unfamiliar word. Even if you can't determine the meaning, you may be able to narrow down the possibilities enough to make a solid guess at the answer to the question.

✓ Prefixes

If you're having trouble with a word in the question or answer choices, try dissecting it. Take advantage of every clue that the word might include. Prefixes can be a huge help. Usually, they allow you to determine a basic meaning. *Pre-* means before, *post-* means after, *pro-* is positive, *de-* is negative. From prefixes, you can get an idea of the general meaning of the word and try to put it into context.

✓ Hedge Words

Watch out for critical hedge words, such as *likely, may, can, often, almost, mostly, usually, generally, rarely*, and *sometimes*. Question writers insert these hedge phrases to cover every possibility. Often an answer choice will be wrong simply because it leaves no room for exception. Be on guard for answer choices that have definitive words such as *exactly* and *always*.

✓ Switchback Words

Stay alert for *switchbacks*. These are the words and phrases frequently used to alert you to shifts in thought. The most common switchback words are *but, although*, and *however*. Others include *nevertheless, on the other hand, even though, while, in spite of, despite*, and *regardless of*. Switchback words are important to catch because they can change the direction of the question or an answer choice.

Copyright © Mometrix Media. You have been licensed one copy of this document for personal use only. Any other reproduction or redistribution is strictly prohibited. All rights reserved.
This content is provided for test preparation purposes only and does not imply an endorsement by Mometrix of any particular political, scientific, or religious point of view.

✓ Face Value

When in doubt, use common sense. Accept the situation in the problem at face value. Don't read too much into it. These problems will not require you to make wild assumptions. If you have to go beyond creativity and warp time or space in order to have an answer choice fit the question, then you should move on and consider the other answer choices. These are normal problems rooted in reality. The applicable relationship or explanation may not be readily apparent, but it is there for you to figure out. Use your common sense to interpret anything that isn't clear.

Answer Choice Strategies

✓ Answer Selection

The most thorough way to pick an answer choice is to identify and eliminate wrong answers until only one is left, then confirm it is the correct answer. Sometimes an answer choice may immediately seem right, but be careful. The test writers will usually put more than one reasonable answer choice on each question, so take a second to read all of them and make sure that the other choices are not equally obvious. As long as you have time left, it is better to read every answer choice than to pick the first one that looks right without checking the others.

✓ Answer Choice Families

An answer choice family consists of two (in rare cases, three) answer choices that are very similar in construction and cannot all be true at the same time. If you see two answer choices that are direct opposites or parallels, one of them is usually the correct answer. For instance, if one answer choice says that quantity *x* increases and another either says that quantity *x* decreases (opposite) or says that quantity *y* increases (parallel), then those answer choices would fall into the same family. An answer choice that doesn't match the construction of the answer choice family is more likely to be incorrect. Most questions will not have answer choice families, but when they do appear, you should be prepared to recognize them.

✓ Eliminate Answers

Eliminate answer choices as soon as you realize they are wrong, but make sure you consider all possibilities. If you are eliminating answer choices and realize that the last one you are left with is also wrong, don't panic. Start over and consider each choice again. There may be something you missed the first time that you will realize on the second pass.

✓ Avoid Fact Traps

Don't be distracted by an answer choice that is factually true but doesn't answer the question. You are looking for the choice that answers the question. Stay focused on what the question is asking for so you don't accidentally pick an answer that is true but incorrect. Always go back to the question and make sure the answer choice you've selected actually answers the question and is not merely a true statement.

✓ Extreme Statements

In general, you should avoid answers that put forth extreme actions as standard practice or proclaim controversial ideas as established fact. An answer choice that states the "process should be used in certain situations, if..." is much more likely to be correct than one that states the "process should be discontinued completely." The first is a calm rational statement and doesn't even make a definitive, uncompromising stance, using a hedge word *if* to provide wiggle room, whereas the second choice is far more extreme.

Copyright © Mometrix Media. You have been licensed one copy of this document for personal use only. Any other reproduction or redistribution is strictly prohibited. All rights reserved.
This content is provided for test preparation purposes only and does not imply an endorsement by Mometrix of any particular political, scientific, or religious point of view.

✓ BENCHMARK

As you read through the answer choices and you come across one that seems to answer the question well, mentally select that answer choice. This is not your final answer, but it's the one that will help you evaluate the other answer choices. The one that you selected is your benchmark or standard for judging each of the other answer choices. Every other answer choice must be compared to your benchmark. That choice is correct until proven otherwise by another answer choice beating it. If you find a better answer, then that one becomes your new benchmark. Once you've decided that no other choice answers the question as well as your benchmark, you have your final answer.

✓ PREDICT THE ANSWER

Before you even start looking at the answer choices, it is often best to try to predict the answer. When you come up with the answer on your own, it is easier to avoid distractions and traps because you will know exactly what to look for. The right answer choice is unlikely to be word-for-word what you came up with, but it should be a close match. Even if you are confident that you have the right answer, you should still take the time to read each option before moving on.

General Strategies

✓ TOUGH QUESTIONS

If you are stumped on a problem or it appears too hard or too difficult, don't waste time. Move on! Remember though, if you can quickly check for obviously incorrect answer choices, your chances of guessing correctly are greatly improved. Before you completely give up, at least try to knock out a couple of possible answers. Eliminate what you can and then guess at the remaining answer choices before moving on.

✓ CHECK YOUR WORK

Since you will probably not know every term listed and the answer to every question, it is important that you get credit for the ones that you do know. Don't miss any questions through careless mistakes. If at all possible, try to take a second to look back over your answer selection and make sure you've selected the correct answer choice and haven't made a costly careless mistake (such as marking an answer choice that you didn't mean to mark). This quick double check should more than pay for itself in caught mistakes for the time it costs.

✓ PACE YOURSELF

It's easy to be overwhelmed when you're looking at a page full of questions; your mind is confused and full of random thoughts, and the clock is ticking down faster than you would like. Calm down and maintain the pace that you have set for yourself. Especially as you get down to the last few minutes of the test, don't let the small numbers on the clock make you panic. As long as you are on track by monitoring your pace, you are guaranteed to have time for each question.

✓ DON'T RUSH

It is very easy to make errors when you are in a hurry. Maintaining a fast pace in answering questions is pointless if it makes you miss questions that you would have gotten right otherwise. Test writers like to include distracting information and wrong answers that seem right. Taking a little extra time to avoid careless mistakes can make all the difference in your test score. Find a pace that allows you to be confident in the answers that you select.

Copyright © Mometrix Media. You have been licensed one copy of this document for personal use only. Any other reproduction or redistribution is strictly prohibited. All rights reserved.
This content is provided for test preparation purposes only and does not imply an endorsement by Mometrix of any particular political, scientific, or religious point of view.

⊘ Keep Moving

Panicking will not help you pass the test, so do your best to stay calm and keep moving. Taking deep breaths and going through the answer elimination steps you practiced can help to break through a stress barrier and keep your pace.

Final Notes

The combination of a solid foundation of content knowledge and the confidence that comes from practicing your plan for applying that knowledge is the key to maximizing your performance on test day. As your foundation of content knowledge is built up and strengthened, you'll find that the strategies included in this chapter become more and more effective in helping you quickly sift through the distractions and traps of the test to isolate the correct answer.

Now that you're preparing to move forward into the test content chapters of this book, be sure to keep your goal in mind. As you read, think about how you will be able to apply this information on the test. If you've already seen sample questions for the test and you have an idea of the question format and style, try to come up with questions of your own that you can answer based on what you're reading. This will give you valuable practice applying your knowledge in the same ways you can expect to on test day.

Good luck and good studying!

Copyright © Mometrix Media. You have been licensed one copy of this document for personal use only. Any other reproduction or redistribution is strictly prohibited. All rights reserved.
This content is provided for test preparation purposes only and does not imply an endorsement by Mometrix of any particular political, scientific, or religious point of view.

Copyright © Mometrix Media. You have been licensed one copy of this document for personal use only. Any other reproduction or redistribution is strictly prohibited. All rights reserved.
This content is provided for test preparation purposes only and does not imply an endorsement by Mometrix of any particular political, scientific, or religious point of view.

Identification and Assessment

Piaget's Stages of Cognitive Development

Sensorimotor Stage

Piaget defined four stages of cognitive development. He called the first stage sensorimotor to characterize infants' cognitive processes: they perceive sensory information from their surrounding environments and respond to these by engaging in motor activities, e.g., rooting, suckling, looking, listening, reaching, and grasping. Piaget divided the sensorimotor stage into six substages: Reflexes, from 0–1 month; Primary Circular Reactions from 1–4 months wherein infants finds accidental actions like thumb-sucking pleasurable and then intentionally repeats them; Secondary Circular Reactions from 4–8 months when infants intentionally repeat actions to evoke environmental effects; Coordination of Reactions from 8–12 months, featuring obviously intentional actions, comprehension of cause and effect, and combining schemas (concepts); Tertiary Circular Reactions from 12–18 months, when children experiment with trial-and-error; and Early Representational Thought from 18–24 months, when children begin representing things or events with symbols. A significant sensorimotor development is Object Permanence, i.e., realizing things still exist when out of sight.

Preoperational Stage

Piaget called his second stage of cognitive development, between the ages of 2–7 years, Preoperational, because children have not yet developed the ability to perform mental operations, i.e., mentally manipulating information, and do not understand concrete logic. Piaget called children in this stage egocentric, i.e., they cannot assume another's perspective. For example, Preoperational children can select a picture matching a three-dimensional scene they just saw, but cannot select a picture matching what someone else would see from a different physical location/position. They do not understand what Piaget termed conservation, the concept that quantities remain constant regardless of shape or appearance. For example, children judge the same amount of liquid differently by its appearance in differently shaped containers (short wide versus tall narrow), even when seeing it poured from one to the other. Piaget identified additional characteristics of Preoperational thinking as animism (attributing human qualities to inanimate objects) and magical thinking (attributing external events to one's internal thoughts).

Concrete Operations Stage

Around ages 7–11 years, children are in what Piaget termed the Concrete Operations stage. A salient feature of this stage is that children develop the ability to think logically and conduct mental operations with regard to concrete objects. However, they still have trouble comprehending hypothetical and abstract concepts. A significant ability developing during this stage is the understanding of reversibility, i.e., that actions can be reversed. Whereas the younger Preoperational child watching someone pour liquid from a short, wide container to a tall, narrow one believes the taller container has more liquid, the Concrete Operations child sees the amount is the same despite different container shapes. Reversibility aids this insight. Children in Concrete Operations also understand sequences between mental categories, e.g., their pet is a poodle, a poodle is a dog, and a dog is an animal. The introduction of formal school subjects, especially math, is no coincidence with the age range of this stage because children in Concrete Operations are first able to do simple arithmetic computations.

Copyright © Mometrix Media. You have been licensed one copy of this document for personal use only. Any other reproduction or redistribution is strictly prohibited. All rights reserved.
This content is provided for test preparation purposes only and does not imply an endorsement by Mometrix of any particular political, scientific, or religious point of view.

Formal Operations

Piaget termed his final stage of cognitive development, from around age 12 into adulthood, as Formal Operations. This reflects the individual's ability to understand and manipulate completely abstract concepts without needing to refer to concrete objects. This stage also features the development of logic, the addition of deductive reasoning to the inductive reasoning children develop in the previous stage of Concrete Operations, and systematic planning. Children/teens/adults can now consider hypothetical situations; apply general principles to predict specific events (deductive reasoning) as well as make generalizations from multiple specific details (inductive reasoning, which typically develops during Concrete Operations); and plan organized, systematic approaches to problem-solving. They are more fully able to consider another's viewpoint and feelings, and can understand abstract concepts like liberty, justice, democracy, truth, and beauty.

Delays in Cognitive Development

Whether caused by neurological deficits or damage, deprivation or other environmental factors, or a combination, some children do not develop cognitive skills typically. They may develop them much later than others or not at all. They may also demonstrate differences in the quantity and quality of their cognitive skills. Children with cognitive developmental delays, for example, can have significant difficulty with learning colors, shapes, and similar basic concepts. They often have trouble learning more advanced concepts, such as counting numbers, reading printed language, and writing language. In addition, children with delayed and/or deficient cognitive development can demonstrate a failure to generalize things they learn to other situations or contexts. Moreover, when children have problems with adjusting to new situations and changes in their environments, this can be a sign of delayed or deficient cognitive development.

Atypical Social and Emotional Development

When children experience developmental delays that are manifested in the social and emotional domain, one characteristic is being too trusting of others, which allows others to take advantage of them. This is often associated with intellectual disability or intellectual disabilities. Another characteristic of some children with atypical social and emotional development is not reading or understanding others' nonverbal cues indicating emotional states or social conventions, and/or linguistic cues during interpersonal interactions, preventing them from responding appropriately. This is commonly associated with autism spectrum disorders. Autistic children also may show excellent verbal skills in monologues, but be unable to initiate and maintain conversations and have difficulty with turn-taking. Some children fail to develop the ability to consider others' viewpoints at typical ages, remaining egocentric; this interferes with social interaction. This is common to various conditions, including intellectual disability, autism, and behavior disorders. Children with ADHD tend to have difficulties with impulse control, emotional self-regulation, and sustaining attention, interfering with social interactions as much as with academic performance.

Atypical Development of Gross Motor Skills

Motor development follows a hierarchical pattern. In other words, for example, if a child cannot stand, s/he cannot walk, and if s/he cannot walk, s/he cannot run. When a baby is between 3 and 12 months old, some signs of atypical gross motor skills development include that the child does not open his/her hands during the normal age range; that the child has trouble holding his/her head up; the child cannot sit up without support, and/or the child has difficulty sitting up even with support; and the child does not begin to pull up on furniture or stand up during this age range. Between 12 and 36 months, signs of delayed/atypical development include problems with walking and/or running; with ascending or descending stairs; with rolling, catching, and throwing a ball;

Copyright © Mometrix Media. You have been licensed one copy of this document for personal use only. Any other reproduction or redistribution is strictly prohibited. All rights reserved.
This content is provided for test preparation purposes only and does not imply an endorsement by Mometrix of any particular political, scientific, or religious point of view.

and with jumping and hopping. Children with atypical motor development may demonstrate higher or lower muscle tone than normal and problems with motor planning, motor coordination, balance, and proprioception.

Fine Motor Skills

Young children need fine motor skills to play with toys, eat meals, turn lights on/off, and hold crayons, paintbrushes, spoons, etc. During evaluations, many children perform poorly on certain tasks, from delays not in cognitive development but in fine motor development. Oral/motor skills, like the control of jaw, lip, mouth, and tongue movements for eating and speaking, are included in fine motor skills. While occupational therapists work with other fine motor skills, speech-language pathologists and occupational therapists may both work to remediate oral/motor skill deficits. If a baby has trouble orally grasping the nipple or bottle to nurse, this can indicate delayed fine motor development. Babies whose hands are in fists more often than open may have fine motor delays. A baby having problems manually bringing toys to his/her mouth and/or mouthing them can have atypical fine motor development. Difficulty holding small objects with a pincer grasp or with a thumb and a forefinger is another sign of delayed fine motor development.

Early Language Development

The development of language skills is critical to the development of cognitive, emotional, and social skills. These are all interrelated, so problems in any one area usually cause problems/delays in others. Receptive language is the ability to understand spoken and written language. Receptive language develops before expressive language: children must understand what they hear before they learn to speak, and to read and comprehend written language before they learn to write. Hence a child's receptive vocabulary typically exceeds his/her expressive vocabulary: s/he can understand more words than s/he can use. Nonverbal receptive language includes understanding others' facial expressions. Verbal receptive language includes understanding what others say; understanding qualitative concepts like big/little and tall/short and quantitative concepts like a lot, a little, all, none, etc.; understanding and following simple directions; listening to stories; understanding and following complex/multiple directions to do a series of things; and understanding others' questions. Written receptive language includes identifying upper- and lowercase letters and numbers, and also reading and comprehending simple and complex sentences and paragraphs.

Receptive, Expressive, and Pragmatic Language and Delayed or Atypical Development

Receptive language is comprehending language we hear and read. Expressive language is our production of spoken and written language. Pragmatic language is our using receptive and expressive language to facilitate social interactions. Expressive and pragmatic language depend upon receptive language, which precedes them. If a baby is not imitating others' vocal sounds or behaviors or responding to hearing his/her name called and/or seems not to be listening to others' speech by the age of 12 months, this can indicate delayed/deficient receptive language development. By three years, if a child does not follow instructions and/or does not learn to speak normally, this can indicate receptive language delay. When children frequently ask others to repeat and/or have trouble answering questions by five years old, they may have receptive language delays. By seven years, signs of receptive language deficits include having trouble understanding stories told/read aloud; avoiding participating in social activities; and having trouble processing or making sense of verbal information. Having trouble reading sentences by nine years old is another sign.

Copyright © Mometrix Media. You have been licensed one copy of this document for personal use only. Any other reproduction or redistribution is strictly prohibited. All rights reserved.
This content is provided for test preparation purposes only and does not imply an endorsement by Mometrix of any particular political, scientific, or religious point of view.

Expressive Language Development

Expressive language is that language we produce in order to communicate with others, whether through spoken or written words, vocal sounds, facial expressions, physical gestures, and/or body language. Babies and children develop expressive language gradually and in a cumulative sequence. Nonverbal expressive language consists of all of that expressive communication that does not involve the use of words. For example, when a baby cries, that is a form of nonverbal expressive language. Smiling also communicates pleasure, recognition, and/or affection toward others. Laughing expresses amusement or delight. Frowning expresses displeasure, sadness, or anger. When infants and toddlers learn to wave "bye-bye," they are using nonverbal expressive language. When babies and young children point at things, they nonverbally communicate a variety of messages—like "I want that"; "Look at that"; "What is that?"; "I see that." When young children throw objects, whether to express anger, protest something, or get an adult to retrieve it as a game, this is also nonverbal expressive language.

Vocal and spoken verbal expressive language in babies and young children: Verbal expressive language can be spoken or written. In infants, early forms of verbalization also include vocalizations. For example, babies "coo" by repeating prolonged vowel sounds; "grunt" or make guttural sounds expressing satisfaction/contentedness; and soon begin to babble by repeating consonant-vowel combinations like "babababa," "dadadada," etc. Babies also imitate adults' vocal sounds and facial expressions. Their first words are often parent names like "Mama" and "Dada," which coincide closely with babbling sounds. As their speech develops, they echo/repeat others' utterances. In the holophrastic stage, toddlers use single words to express phrase concepts, like "up" to mean "Pick me up" or "Look at the bird up there." They combine pointing with nouns to identify people, animals, and things, like "baby," "doggie," or "car." They soon learn to use the socially conventional utterances "thank you" and "please." Toddlers then learn to combine two words to express phrase concepts, like "Daddy go" or "Mommy shoe," which can also convey a variety of meanings.

Development of spoken verbal expressive language skills: Once they can speak using more than one-word expressions, young children begin to ask questions and answer others' questions. They progress to correctly using words expressing qualitative concepts, including opposites like big and little, tall and short, etc.; and quantitative concepts, including opposite and relative quantities like all, none, a lot, or a little. As their expressive language skills develop, they reflect children's receptive understanding of the concepts underlying the words. The toddler's basic "She walk" phrase gives way to the more advanced present progressive verb tense "She is walking" in preschoolers. Children begin to use pronouns like "I" and "you," rather than using no pronouns or only "me" or "Mommy." They then develop possessive pronouns like "mine" and "my" [+ object]. They start including prepositions like on, in, over, and under. They use past tenses, both regular and irregular ("gave") and future constructions like "will/is going to" [+verb]. They progress from two-word to three- and four-word phrases, and then full sentences with subject, auxiliary verb, verb, and object.

Activities that reflect written expressive language skills development: Children learn to speak before they learn to write, though there is also some overlap in their developing spoken and written expressive language skills. These both also depend on the development of the receptive language skills of listening and reading comprehension. Young children first learn to trace letters, then they copy them, and then they write them. They follow the same progression with tracing, copying, and writing numbers. They copy examples of simple words, like "Mom," and then do the same with more complex words like "truck." Once they have copied words and can remember letters, they progress to writing the letters in sequence to spell written words (d-a-d-d-y). Thereafter, they learn

Copyright © Mometrix Media. You have been licensed one copy of this document for personal use only. Any other reproduction or redistribution is strictly prohibited. All rights reserved.
This content is provided for test preparation purposes only and does not imply an endorsement by Mometrix of any particular political, scientific, or religious point of view.

to write consecutive words that form sentences, such as "I love my kitty." Eventually, school-age children can write connected sentences that form paragraphs, like "I love my kitty. One day my friends will come over. I will show my kitty to my friends."

Signs in babies and young children are of atypical development or delays: Babies normally babble at a few to several months. An infant's not babbling by eight months is a sign of delayed/atypical spoken language development. A child not uttering any words by 18 months is not developing expressive language normally. Children over two years using only single words show atypical development. After four years, speaking mainly in "baby talk" is atypical. Echolalia (continually repeating what others say) is normal in younger children, but beyond three years is atypical. Talking to oneself aloud is typical of toddlers, but children continuing this practice extensively past three years show delayed development. Children older than three years who do not take conversational turns but talk "in circles" are not developing typically. Children over four years who have trouble expressing their needs and wants show atypical development. Answering open-ended questions ("What did you do at Jimmy's?") with single words indicates a delay in a six-year-old. Overgeneralizing, i.e., naming many objects with one word like calling all vehicles cars, is another sign of delayed expressive language development.

Babies who make no, or very little, eye contact with others by 12 months of age are not developing typically. Another sign indicating a need for evaluation is not pointing at things by this age. Children who demonstrate few or no skills at taking turns by a year old can have expressive language delays. Little or no demonstration of joint attention, i.e., attending to the same thing as his/her parent, is another sign of developmental delay. So is a lack of joint action, i.e., engaging in the same activity as the parent. Children who consistently hit others or have temper tantrums when they cannot communicate a message to others show signs of delayed expressive language. Crying, yelling, and similar shows of frustration when trying to communicate also indicate developmental delays. In addition, young children with such delays may rarely if ever initiate conversations with others, and may not want to engage in activities with others.

Physical and Motor Development of Children with Down Syndrome

Children with Down syndrome show overall slower development in physiology and motor skills. They grow more slowly in physical size and also ultimately attain smaller full statures than typically developing children. They tend to have lower/weaker muscle tone, or hypotonia. They commonly start walking significantly later than other children. Even once they learn to walk, they may not develop physical coordination, balance, and proprioception as soon or ever as well as other children. The oral-motor skills components of motor development are also slower to develop in those with Down syndrome, compounded by having large, thick, often protruding tongues, which can interfere with eating skills and clear speech. Additional physiological stigmata of Down syndrome include small hands and feet; short, stubby fingers; short, thick necks; small heads, flattened in back; small noses; and Asian-appearing eyes with epicanthal folds. Down syndrome children are more likely to have celiac disease (gluten intolerance), gastroesophageal reflux, hypothyroidism, hearing and vision problems, and to develop senile dementias earlier than normally.

Development of Students with Autism Spectrum Disorders

Language

An estimated one-half of those on the autism spectrum never develop verbal language skills. The other half range from echolalia as their only speech production to perfectly functional, high-level speech, and everything in between. Some autistic students display advanced vocabularies and fluent speech in long monologues about topics interesting them, often including the highly

Copyright © Mometrix Media. You have been licensed one copy of this document for personal use only. Any other reproduction or redistribution is strictly prohibited. All rights reserved.
This content is provided for test preparation purposes only and does not imply an endorsement by Mometrix of any particular political, scientific, or religious point of view.

specialized and/or technical, but are unable to initiate or maintain two-way conversations with others. These individuals have difficulty with turn-taking and the give-and-take of verbal interactions. Some high-functioning autistic persons can conduct normal conversations with others, but their speech patterns may sound a bit singsong, odd, or quirky. Many autistic students have difficulty understanding emotional overtones in others' speech, such as sarcasm or humor. Additionally, they often cannot understand nonverbal cues like facial expressions, gestures, and body language indicating emotions or social customs, though many can learn this through explicit training.

SOCIAL AND EMOTIONAL

Emotional and social differences can be observed in autistic people from early childhood, when many of them avoid eye contact with others and resist physical contact with parents, like flinging themselves backward from being hugged/held or going rigid in their bodies when held. Many also engage in repetitive, stereotypic self-stimulating behaviors like rocking. Students with autism experience the same internal emotions as others, but may not express these normally. Moreover, they often have great difficulty noticing or understanding the emotions of others and their expression of them. As a result, their behavior in social situations can appear rather strange, especially from high-functioning autistic individuals with above-average intelligence. For example, as autism expert John Gerdtz once related, "It's really strange when you're talking with someone who has a PhD in mathematics, and he suddenly turns and walks away right in the middle of the conversation." Autistic individuals frequently fail to follow social conventions because they do not understand them.

BEHAVIORAL DIFFERENCES

One area of behavioral difference among the autistic is language: some people with autism spectrum disorders (ASDs) have few or no verbal skills; others have limited speech and language; others have more functional, but odd-sounding speech and language; and still others have highly functioning verbal skills. Some are able to speak extensively on favorite topics but cannot start or continue social conversations. Another area is social and emotional: those with ASDs have difficulty observing, interpreting, and using socially accepted behaviors indicating emotions. A common autistic deficit is tolerating interruptions, changes, or transitions in activities. Autistic people frequently display narrowly limited interests and activities, and rigid thinking and behavior. The lower functioning often engage in repetitive behaviors; the higher functioning can focus intensely on a single activity for long periods, but not shift or divide their attention. Some autistic individuals react to sudden changes, or sensory input they find painful due to hypersensitivity, with panic reactions including screaming, self-injurious behavior, and/or withdrawal into rocking, counting, or other repetitive self-soothing actions.

DEAF STUDENTS

DIFFERENCES IN LEARNING

Hearing children are surrounded by speech sounds from birth, and they absorb a great deal of their knowledge and understanding of language and speech through this immersion. However, deaf children do not benefit from sensory input in the auditory mode. Those whose parents use sign language and/or speech reading learn to comprehend and produce language through the visual modality instead. This is a major difference, because the main basis for communication among the majority of the population is auditory; and written language, with its relationship to spoken language, has the same auditory basis. Instead of auditory cues like tone of voice, grammatical inflections (like verb tense or plural endings), or intonations like the rising end of a question, deaf students rely exclusively on visual cues like facial expressions, gestures, and body language; and in ASL (American Sign Language), built-in signs conveying grammatical information.

Copyright © Mometrix Media. You have been licensed one copy of this document for personal use only. Any other reproduction or redistribution is strictly prohibited. All rights reserved.
This content is provided for test preparation purposes only and does not imply an endorsement by Mometrix of any particular political, scientific, or religious point of view.

Similarities to Hearing Students

Although a major difference in deaf students is that they learn language through visual rather than auditory modalities, they also have many similarities to hearing students. They have the same need to communicate and interact socially with others. Unfortunately, the majority of hearing people do not know sign language; and while many deaf people can visually read speech, many others who sign exclusively and adhere to deaf culture function best within the signing deaf community and are at significant disadvantages in hearing milieus. While deaf students often do not understand humor based on word play or sound, they do appreciate humor, and the deaf culture has its own inside jokes. Deaf students have equal interests in competing in sports and academics as hearing students do. They feel the same emotions as others. While they hug each other more and spend longer times on good-byes, their social interactions still fulfill the same needs for belonging, connection, and communication.

Blind Students

Differences from Sighted Students

Blind students with normal hearing do not miss out on the auditory medium wherein children learn to understand and use speech and language as deaf students do. However, while they can learn spoken language normally, they cannot learn to read and write visually as other children can. They must learn Braille and have access to Braille publications to read and/or listen to books on tape. Today they have the added advantage of computer text-to-speech software. Another significant difference is that blind students cannot learn their way around schools and other large, complex buildings simply through the experience of navigating them a few times. Sighted individuals often take this for granted. Blind students usually need help from Orientation and Mobility specialists to learn how to get around in indoor and outdoor settings. Without the benefit of the multitude of visual information others have, it can be very confusing not to know just which way to go, but even where one is and in what position relative to one's surroundings (orientation).

Similarities to Sighted Individuals

Although the totally blind cannot read printed text, blind students still often want to read and enjoy it. Some read available Braille texts by touch. Others listen to books on tape and/or use text-to-speech computer software, greatly expanding their options of available texts. Though blind students may not understand visual humor like sight gags, they still appreciate humor. Students not blind from birth have additional frames of reference for understanding visual expressions and comparisons. For example, Helen Keller, who became deaf-blind at 19 months, reportedly was told she had blue eyes and asked, "Are they like wee skies?" Without hearing or sight, Keller had to learn tactile finger-spelling to communicate, yet her accomplishments made her famous. A woman who became blind around nine years old found hilarious a coworker's description of another employee bundled up in a fur coat and hat with only her nose protruding. Blind people have the same social, communication, and emotional needs; they just need supplementary auditory information/verbal descriptions of what they cannot see.

Differences and Similarities of Physically Disabled Students

Physically normal students, and sometimes even educators, may not realize that even navigating through a school building—a seemingly simple everyday activity they take for granted—is not the same for the physically disabled. For example, buildings with traditional construction frequently include doorways too narrow for wheelchairs, solid obstacles impossible or difficult to move around, or stairs and grades not safely traversed using crutches. Federal legislation protecting the rights of the disabled has now mandated that all new constructions be accessible to them; however, this does not address old/existing buildings that often cannot be retrofitted. Also, physically

Copyright © Mometrix Media. You have been licensed one copy of this document for personal use only. Any other reproduction or redistribution is strictly prohibited. All rights reserved.
This content is provided for test preparation purposes only and does not imply an endorsement by Mometrix of any particular political, scientific, or religious point of view.

disabled students have the same needs and desires to compete, win, and play as others, which should not be discounted. For example, wheelchair basketball and races are popular alternatives. In some schools, students in wheelchairs are also included in regular sports teams and games.

Family's Role

Families play a critical role by frequently serving as their disabled child's first case manager. In this capacity, they are the most consistent and know the most about their child's abilities and needs. Families help coordinate the services disabled children need. They help them explore career possibilities and interests. They supply housing, transportation, adaptive equipment, and other necessities. When young people with disabilities progress from high school to college or employment and community living, their families support the transitions they must make. Families can help their children achieve greater understanding of themselves and their disabilities. However, many families do not realize how crucial such self-knowledge is, and many assume the schools teach this when they seldom do. Also, when educators and families avoid directly discussing disabilities and focus instead on abilities and strengths, children can grow up not realizing their disability's impact and the accommodations to facilitate their success. Students who avoid identification as disabled for fear of labeling and stigma are frequently unprepared for self-advocacy.

Understanding, Communication, and Disclosure of Disability

Young people with disabilities will benefit by learning to understand themselves more fully; to understand their disabilities more completely; and to explain their disabilities more effectively to others. They will often need help from experts to make decisions whether to disclose their disability to others and to become more prepared for such disclosure. Even more importantly, young people with disabilities need to gain a better comprehension of how their opportunities in social, educational, and employment contexts can often be enhanced by disclosing their disabilities in certain situations. Where appropriate, disclosure of disability can give them access to services and accommodations they would not be entitled to if they were not disabled. Experts have prepared informational publications to support them in this issue. For example, the National Collaborative on Workforce and Disability for Youth (NCWD-Y) has published *The 411 on Disability Disclosure: A Workbook for Youth with Disabilities* to help youth and parents make informed decisions about disclosure and its various impacts.

Financial and Service Challenges on Family Systems

The challenges and demands on family systems are compounded when a member has a disability, and such challenges are typically long-term. Regardless of the type of family, the age of the disabled member, and the type of disability, many of the family demands are the same. For example, obtaining appropriate health services, social services, and educational services of sufficient quality often entail significant economic burdens, as do modifying the home to accommodate a disability and procuring adaptive equipment, medications, and special diets. Although families may qualify for public funding, e.g., from Medicaid, Social Security SSI, or private health insurance, additional challenges are not only to discover which programs and services their child is eligible for, but moreover to interact with various bureaucracies to confirm such eligibility—frequently on a repeated basis. Another major problem is service coordination among providers, like doctors, teachers, counselors, physical and occupational therapists, social workers, and dietitians. Frequently providers are not informed of one another's actions and may give contradictory information.

Copyright © Mometrix Media. You have been licensed one copy of this document for personal use only. Any other reproduction or redistribution is strictly prohibited. All rights reserved.
This content is provided for test preparation purposes only and does not imply an endorsement by Mometrix of any particular political, scientific, or religious point of view.

Impact on Families

Emotional and Caregiving

Caring for a disabled child or family member, particularly one with more severe disabilities, is a daily stressor that can exhaust caregivers and all family members emotionally and physically. Emotional stress includes anxiety, anger, guilt, and insecurity—about the disability's cause, other family members' needs, whether caregivers are doing enough, the future, etc. Families grieve the disabled member's functional losses, initially and recurrently. A member's disability frequently causes major changes in family life. Members, especially females, may discard or alter jobs and/or career plans for caregiving duties. Some members feel too involved in care while others feel left out, and within-family relationships change. Different loyalties and/or alliances develop within the family. Past research has found that while disability tended to increase marital tension, it did not necessarily increase divorce rates.

Family Resources, Social Roles, Lifestyle, Leisure Time, and Community Interactions

When a family member has a disability, it can deplete the family's resources in terms of money, time, and energy far out of proportion to other demands. This often detracts from meeting other needs of the family and its other members. The family members find they must change their lifestyle, for example, spending less money, time, and energy on leisure activities and staying at home more. Families may abandon their plans and dreams for the future because they no longer have enough of these resources to pursue them. Community members may exclude the disabled member and family; avoid them; and/or denigrate them with looks or comments. Though federal legislation mandates inclusion, many communities do not have the resources, facilities, and programs to enable full inclusion. Many families state they feel burdened not by the disabled member, but by rejection, judgment, stigmatization of the member and family, and other negative behaviors and attitudes—from not only strangers, but also service providers, friends, and relatives.

Variation in the Impact of Disabilities on Families

Research shows the functioning and health of family members can be compromised by disability's additional demands. This includes elevated risks of behavioral and psychological symptoms in other family members. But despite this greater risk, studies also find that the majority of children and adults in families with a disabled member do not demonstrate such behavioral or psychological problems. This is attributed to the family members' adaptive abilities: they find and apply various coping skills to address the additional stresses caused in their life by the disability. Even though having a disabled member can cause families to experience grief, fatigue, depletion of resources, and other stressors, many families have also reported experiencing greater family closeness, acceptance of other people, new friendships, deepened spiritual faith, greater self-efficacy and sense of competence, more respect for life, and becoming stronger as a family. Thus, both negative and positive consequences are associated with having a family member with a disability.

Differential Psychosocial Effects

Families are affected differentially by the degree of a member's disability: its type, i.e., whether it is a motor, sensory, or cognitive disability; how visible the disability is; how much pain or other symptoms are involved; the disabled member's life expectancy or prognosis; how much treatment and/or care is required; and whether the disability is progressive, constant, or relapsing in nature. Some experts believe these characteristics have more influence on a chronic condition's psychosocial impact than the diagnosis itself. Constant disabilities, e.g., spinal cord injuries, necessitate major initial family restructuring, plus long-term endurance and persistence. While the family can plan for a known future, they can still become exhausted, especially if community resources are lacking. Progressive disabilities, e.g., dementia or degenerative arthritis, cause grief

Copyright © Mometrix Media. You have been licensed one copy of this document for personal use only. Any other reproduction or redistribution is strictly prohibited. All rights reserved.
This content is provided for test preparation purposes only and does not imply an endorsement by Mometrix of any particular political, scientific, or religious point of view.

over continuous losses, uncertainty about living arrangements and degrees of dependency, and increasing demands in caretaking. Relapsing disabilities, e.g., cancer or epilepsy, require less continual care but more ability to shift suddenly from normal to crisis mode and rapidly activate resources.

Differential Impacts of Cognitive or Intellectual Disabilities

Research studies have shown that families appear to have more difficulty coping with cognitive or intellectual disabilities. Mental impairments can limit the disabled member's ability to assume responsible roles or to live independently, and/or increase the demands on families to be more vigilant to protect the disabled member. In cases of severe or profound intellectual disability, families may experience additional stress caused by boundary ambiguity—i.e., the disparity between the disabled member's physical and psychological presence makes his or her membership in the family unclear to the other members, as the disabled member is present as a part of the family in some ways, but in other ways is absent or only partially present. The ambiguity of this situation causes families more stress, as it can be more difficult for them to plan the roles of the other family members when they do not know what they can expect.

Effects of Medical Advances

When the life expectancy of a disabled member is unclear, the family finds it harder to plan its members' future roles in life; to know future care costs; or, when the member needs help with daily living activities, to decide on optimal living arrangements. For example, individuals with Down syndrome often have congenital heart defects and died younger in the past, but with improved medical care, they now live longer. And between 1970 and 1991, the survival of American children with cystic fibrosis increased by 700 percent, from a median life expectancy of eight years to twenty-six years. This opens up new questions about marriage, procreation, and other difficult family choices. Ethical problems are also presented when medical advances can extend the lives of those with serious medical conditions. Considerations include weighing benefits versus costs, when and/or why to intervene and how aggressively. Family members may disagree about these. Moreover, courts and/or hospitals may prohibit chosen family actions. Such cases provoke much controversy (witness the 1998–2005 case of Terri Schiavo).

Considerations for Families Regarding Functional Status

A person's functional status is the extent to which s/he can perform activities of daily living (ADLs) like self-feeding, toileting, or walking. The severity of impairment in these activities caused by a disability can be assessed. The human help, support, and equipment an individual will require is inversely related to his/her functional status, and families are typically the main providers of such assistance. Providing it can constitute a burden for them, compromising their physical and mental health. For instance, research has found that parents and particularly mothers whose disabled children have lower functional status have more symptoms of depression. Another factor to consider is that when disabled children and their parents both grow older, and/or when grandparents are caregivers, their ability to provide the same amounts and durations of care can become more limited due to the physical stresses of caregiving, which may be unmanageable for many elderly persons.

Significance of Age of Disability Onset and the Age of Parents at Onset or Diagnosis

In contrast to disabilities manifested in late adulthood, which are more predictable and less disruptive psychologically to families, disabilities occurring earlier in life are perceived as less normal, affect development more, and require making more adjustments for longer times. Congenital disabilities shape the identity and life of a child, so the child and family are not required

Copyright © Mometrix Media. You have been licensed one copy of this document for personal use only. Any other reproduction or redistribution is strictly prohibited. All rights reserved.
This content is provided for test preparation purposes only and does not imply an endorsement by Mometrix of any particular political, scientific, or religious point of view.

to adjust to a sudden loss of function. An example is the difference between a child born with spina bifida versus a normal adolescent who sustains an injury and suddenly becomes paraplegic. Parental age at onset is also a factor in family response to disability. Adolescent parents still have salient developmental needs themselves; plus, they usually have fewer resources and less maturity for coping with the additional demands of their child's disability. Older parents have greater risks of bearing children with Down syndrome and other disabilities, lesser endurance for caregiving, and more fears about who will care for their child after their deaths.

Interrelationship of Disability and Child Development

Because childhood development is sequential, the mastery of skills at each level or stage depends upon the successful completion of the previous stage. Therefore, the earlier in a child's life the onset of a disabling condition is, the more it interrupts the child's developmental progress. Accomplishing developmental tasks is complicated in many ways for children with disabilities. This influences what family roles the child can adopt and consequently affects the family. If an infant's disability prevents the infant from responding to parental efforts at nurturing, this impedes the development of bonding, secure attachment, and trust, undermining parenting competence. Toddlers must actively explore their social environments to develop self-control and autonomy. But sensory, motor, or cognitive disabilities can hamper such exploration. Parents may be overprotective for fear of additional damage or injury, and/or, due to guilt or sympathy, overindulgent. Others' negative feedback about the child's disability can reinforce these parental behaviors, additionally limiting the child's development of self-control and autonomy.

Challenges with Attending School

As Freud, Erikson, Piaget, and others have observed, when children begin school, their social and emotional focus shifts from the parent-child relationship to developing social relationships outside of the home with peers, children of other ages, and adults other than parents. The focus of child development consequently shifts from mainly personal skills and parental attachment to social competencies and interpersonal skills. In spite of government mandates of special education and inclusion, schools still vary significantly in their effectiveness with these. Insufficient funding for special education programs; inadequate training of school staff for accommodating instruction to special needs; and frequently, negative attitudes regarding disabilities in school personnel and other children, constitute some of the obstacles faced by children with disabilities and their parents. Because of the variance among schools in this respect, some families realize great resources in school programs, while others realize great additional challenges in trying to advocate for their disabled children's educational rights with schools and other service providers.

Challenges of Adolescent Development

As especially elucidated by Erikson, adolescents have the developmental tasks of developing their individual identities, separating from their childhood relationships with parents, and becoming more independent. Having a disability makes these tasks more challenging for a teenager. While normally developing adolescents often engage in risk-taking, e.g., experimenting with alcohol and tobacco, as part of this process, teens with disabilities may refuse prescribed medications, diets, or other disability-related treatments as their form of the risk-taking part of the developmental process. The natural adolescent development of sexuality also involves additional complications for disabled teens, as they often experience anxieties and fears about their desirability, performance, and future potential for marriage and reproduction. The complications they encounter can include being exploited sexually by others for the cognitively disabled, risk of contracting sexually transmitted diseases, and possible higher risks of pregnancy for girls with disabilities.

Copyright © Mometrix Media. You have been licensed one copy of this document for personal use only. Any other reproduction or redistribution is strictly prohibited. All rights reserved.
This content is provided for test preparation purposes only and does not imply an endorsement by Mometrix of any particular political, scientific, or religious point of view.

Amphetamines for ADHD

Many adults do not understand why a child who is already hyperactive would be prescribed a stimulant drug, thinking this would only make them even more so. However, stimulants like amphetamines often have the effect of helping children with ADHD to focus their attention better for longer time periods. This compares to the effects of caffeine and controlled amphetamine doses in helping normal but tired adults concentrate better. Serious amphetamine side effects include rapid, uneven, or pounding heartbeat; burning or pain with urination; increased talkativeness; other unaccustomed behaviors; extremes of depression or elation; muscular twitches/motor tics; physical tremors; hallucinations; and dangerous elevations in blood pressure, with symptoms like buzzing in the ears, severe headaches, shortness of breath, cardiac arrhythmias, chest pain, confusion, anxiety, seizures, and others. Less serious side effects include blurred vision, dizziness, weakness, moderate headaches, irritability, restlessness, agitation, insomnia, dry mouth, bad taste in the mouth, constipation, diarrhea, stomachache, nausea, vomiting, fever, loss of appetite, weight loss, hair loss, loss of libido, and others.

Depakote

Depakote is an anticonvulsive prescribed to control seizures. It can sometimes cause pancreatitis or liver damage. If so, symptoms include jaundice, low-grade fever, pale/clay-colored stools, dark-colored urine, loss of appetite, upper stomach pain, nausea, and vomiting. Emergency medical attention should be pursued if the child has these symptoms. Additional serious side effects include agitation, anxiety, depression, hostility, mental or physical hyperactivity, restlessness, suicidal or self-injurious ideations, confusion, fainting, weakness, bruising easily, urine in the blood, body aches, swollen glands, other flu-like symptoms, decreased urination, excessive sleepiness, incoordination, nystagmus, double vision, painful skin, burning eyes, rashes with blisters and peeling, and other symptoms. Allergic reactions to Depakote cause symptoms of breathing difficulty, hives, and/or swelling of the throat, tongue, lips, or face. Less serious side effects include mild sleepiness, mild weakness, upset stomach, constipation, diarrhea, tremors, changes in vision, hair loss, an unpleasant/unusual taste in the mouth, and others. Educators should always know students are taking seizure medications. They should not first assume behavior or mental disorders or sleep deprivation.

Pulmozyme

A doctor may prescribe Pulmozyme to a patient who has cystic fibrosis. This condition causes thick mucus secretions in the lungs, interfering with normal breathing. Excessive DNA in the pulmonary secretions causes these symptoms. Pulmozyme is a synthesized protein that breaks down this extra DNA. It makes the lung secretions thinner and thus less likely to obstruct breathing, and also decreases the patient's risk of respiratory tract infections. Pulmozyme is given in solution via inhalation from a nebulizer. Allergic reactions to Pulmozyme cause symptoms like breathing difficulty, swelling of the face, lips, or tongue, hives, swelling/closing of the throat, chest pain, and/or fever. Emergency medical attention or immediate physician contact are indicated for these, which are the primary serious side effects. Less serious Pulmozyme side effects include changes in the voice; a sore throat; laryngitis; rashes; conjunctivitis, or red, irritated, or inflamed eyes; nasal congestion and/or discharge; and other symptoms, for which a doctor should be consulted.

Medications for Childhood Anxiety Disorders

According to psychiatrists, children with anxiety are often prescribed the wrong medications when practitioners fail to understand the children's experiences and lack knowledge of evidence-based anxiety treatments. Anxious children have attentional difficulties, not from attention deficits but worries. They are often misdiagnosed as having ADHD and prescribed stimulants. These improve

Copyright © Mometrix Media. You have been licensed one copy of this document for personal use only. Any other reproduction or redistribution is strictly prohibited. All rights reserved.
This content is provided for test preparation purposes only and does not imply an endorsement by Mometrix of any particular political, scientific, or religious point of view.

concentration, but not mood; they can even increase anxiety and the insomnia it causes. Alpha-two agonists, e.g., clonidine or guanfacine, lower arousal levels and can calm children, but do not treat their anxiety. Some practitioners even prescribe antipsychotics, also inappropriate for anxiety disorders. Serotonin-specific reuptake inhibitor (SSRI) antidepressants are most effective in research studies and patient treatments by experienced psychiatric physicians. These can improve children's anxiety relatively fast, e.g., beginning in a week or two, and are most effective in conjunction with cognitive-behavior therapy. Benzodiazepines (Valium, Librium, Dalmane, Halcion, Xanax, Ativan, etc.), used as anti-seizure treatments, sleep aids, and muscle relaxants as well as anxiolytics, also provide short-term help for extreme anxiety, but not long-term help like SSRIs.

Medications for Childhood Schizophrenia

While the symptoms of childhood schizophrenia can differ from adult symptoms, the same antipsychotic medications are prescribed to children as adults (though in different dosages), in conjunction with psychotherapy. A few of these drugs include Haldol, Thorazine, Stelazine, Mellaril, Risperdal, Loxitane, Moban, and lithium, which is also often prescribed for bipolar disorder. Antipsychotics in the phenothiazine class, such as Thorazine, Stelazine, and Mellaril, have significant risks of side effects like tardive dyskinesia, which refers to repetitive, involuntary movements that can be irreversible even upon discontinuing treatment; dystonias, like involuntary tongue thrusts, muscular rigidity, etc.; and extrapyramidal syndrome, involving muscle spasms, which are usually reversible on discontinuing treatment but may need other treatments to resolve when they are serious or interfere with breathing. Another side effect is pseudoparkinsonism, which mimics the symptoms of Parkinson disease including "pill-rolling" finger tremors, "mask-like" flat facial appearance, a shuffling gait, and muscular rigidity. A very serious side effect is neuroleptic malignant syndrome. Thorazine and other phenothiazines can also themselves cause psychiatric side effects.

Gabapentin

Although gabapentin is prescribed to adults for the nerve pain of shingles and for Restless Legs Syndrome, it is prescribed to children primarily for seizure disorders. For epilepsy, it is prescribed alone or with other medications to children at least 12 years old as well as adults, and with other medications to children aged 3–12 years for partial seizures. Caution is advised with patients having liver disease, kidney disease, or heart disease. Gabapentin can cause suicidal or self-injurious ideations in some patients. It can also cause depression, anxiety, changes in mood or behavior, agitation, hostility, restlessness, or physical or mental hyperactivity. Serious gabapentin side effects include increased instead of decreased seizures; fever, body aches, swollen glands, flu-like symptoms; bleeding or bruising easily; skin rashes; severe tingling, numbness, or pain; muscular weakness; chest pain, heart arrhythmia, shortness of breath; rapid weight gain, edema/swelling; less/no urination; confusion; nausea, vomiting; worsened/new coughing; difficulty breathing; nystagmus; and upper stomach pain, loss of appetite, dark urine, and jaundice (signs of liver damage).

Gabapentin is prescribed to children to control seizures. It is also prescribed to adults for Restless Legs Syndrome and for nerve pain secondary to shingles. It may be prescribed to some children for whom other anti-seizure medications have not been effective. Some less serious side effects of gabapentin include sleepiness, dizziness, weakness, fatigue; constipation, diarrhea, nausea; blurred vision; headaches; swelling of the breasts; dryness of the mouth; and loss of coordination or balance. In children particularly, gabapentin is more likely to cause problems with memory, changes in behavior, difficulty concentrating, and restless, aggressive, or hostile behavior. If parents or caregivers observe any of these side effects in children who are taking gabapentin, they should always contact the prescribing physician. Educators should always ensure they are informed when

Copyright © Mometrix Media. You have been licensed one copy of this document for personal use only. Any other reproduction or redistribution is strictly prohibited. All rights reserved.
This content is provided for test preparation purposes only and does not imply an endorsement by Mometrix of any particular political, scientific, or religious point of view.

students are taking seizure medications, especially younger children less likely to know/understand or volunteer this information. They should not automatically assume a child has an attention deficit or behavior disorder instead. They should also realize this is probably the reason if a student seems sleepy.

Medical Needs for Spina Bifida

Spina bifida is a neural tube defect: the neural tube that will become the baby's brain, spinal cord, and enclosing tissues does not close completely. Of its several types, spina bifida occulta frequently needs no treatment. Spina bifida meningocele requires surgery to replace the meninges back into the spinal column and close the vertebral opening. Spina bifida myelomeningocele needs surgery within 24 to 48 hours of birth to lessen infection risk and protect the spinal cord from further trauma. Surgeons sometimes install a shunt in the infant's brain during surgery to control hydrocephalus, a buildup of fluid in the brain. Fetal surgery, before week 26 of gestation, reduces children's needs for brain shunts, crutches/walkers/braces, etc., but is risky for mothers and highly elevates premature birth risk. Despite early surgery, children with myelomeningocele often have lower-body paralysis and bladder and bowel problems. Treatment includes exercises preparing for later assisted walking. Myelomeningocele complications include tethered spinal cord from postoperative scar tissue, inhibiting growth. Surgery can restore some function and mitigate the extent of disability

Medical Needs for Muscular Dystrophy

Muscular dystrophy, a genetic condition, makes muscle fibers unusually vulnerable to damage, causing progressive weakness. Symptoms include breathing/swallowing difficulties and limb contractures. Some forms affect the heart and other organs. Among at least seven forms of MD, the Duchenne type comprises roughly half of all cases and is most common in boys. Children learning to walk may fall often; have trouble getting up, running, and jumping; waddle when walking; and have enlarged calf muscles. They also often have learning disabilities. With no cure, treatment focuses on decreasing/preventing spinal and joint deformities and enabling mobility as long as possible. Prednisone and other corticosteroids can slow progression of some forms of MD and enhance muscular strength, but also weaken bones, elevating fracture risks, with long-term use. Surgeries can loosen contracted joints, correct spinal scoliosis to ease breathing, and install pacemakers for MD-related heart conditions. Range-of-motion exercises improve flexibility. Braces support weak muscles, stretch muscles and tendons, and preserve flexibility, slowing contracture progression. Some patients need C-PAP sleep apnea devices or ventilators.

Medical Needs for Cystic Fibrosis

Children who inherit cystic fibrosis have a genetic defect that makes normally thin, slippery secretory juices become thick and sticky. These fluids, which normally lubricate the tissues, when thickened obstruct passageways, ducts, and tubes, particularly in the lungs and pancreas. CF has no cure, and treatment involves complex management. However, improved detection and intervention have decreased complications and ameliorated symptoms, allowing children to live longer. Treatment focuses on loosening and eliminating mucus from the lungs; preventing and controlling lung infections; preventing and treating intestinal obstructions; and supplying sufficient nutrition. This includes antibiotics; mucus-thinning medications; bronchodilators to keep airways open; pancreatic enzymes to improve nutrient absorption; chest clapping by hand or mechanical device, inflatable vibrating vests, and breathing masks/tubes; breathing exercises and strategies; nutritional counseling; energy-conserving techniques; counseling, and/or support groups. Additional procedures include oxygen therapy to prevent pulmonary hypertension, endoscopy and lavage to suction mucus, surgical nasal polyp removal, feeding tubes for supplemental nutrition, surgical removal of bowel obstructions, and lung transplants.

Copyright © Mometrix Media. You have been licensed one copy of this document for personal use only. Any other reproduction or redistribution is strictly prohibited. All rights reserved.
This content is provided for test preparation purposes only and does not imply an endorsement by Mometrix of any particular political, scientific, or religious point of view.

Treatments Addressing Medical Needs of Cerebral Palsy

Damage or deficient development in the brain before birth usually causes cerebral palsy, which affects muscle tone, posture, and movement. It can include spasticity causing muscular rigidity and incoordination, athetosis causing involuntary movements and exaggerated reflexes, or both. Its effects can range from an unsteady gait or slight limp to complete loss of walking and speech, and every degree in between these. Botox can help isolated spasticity, and muscle relaxants can help generalized spasticity. CP patients benefit from physical therapy to improve motor development, mobility, strength, balance, and flexibility. Splints or braces can stretch stiff muscles, prevent contractures, and help some children walk. Occupational therapists provide adaptive equipment and alternate strategies to help children participate independently in daily routines and activities. Speech-language therapists help children speak clearly, use sign language or communication boards/devices, and improve eating/swallowing muscle use. Orthopedic surgery for severe deformities or contractures can reposition bones or joints; lengthen contracted tendons and muscles to reduce pain and increase mobility; and sometimes sever extremely spastic muscles.

Reliability and Validity

Reliability is consistency of an assessment instrument's data across repeated administrations. For example, reliable test scores are similar when the same test-taker is given the test two/three times at two-week intervals. Internal consistency reliability is consistency of test items with one another by measuring the same quantity/construct. Inter-rater consistency is reliability among individuals scoring the same test. Intra-rater consistency is an individual's consistency in rating responses to various test items. Validity is whether a test measures what it claims/intends to measure. Content validity means a test includes items representing the complete range of possible items. Construct validity means a test's scores measure the construct they are meant to measure, like intelligence. Criterion validity means a test's scores effectively measure a construct according to established criteria. Concurrent validity, a type of criterion validity, means a test measures the criterion and the construct at the same time. Predictive validity, another type of criterion validity, means test scores effectively predict future outcomes, as when aptitude tests predict future subject grades.

Generalizability, Compensatory Grading, Noncompensatory Grading, and Cut Score

Generalizability is related to reliability, i.e., the consistency of test scores over repeated administrations; but it moreover refers to the specific features of a certain test administration. It means the results on one test can be generalized to apply to other tests with similar formats, content, and operations. Generalizability can also refer to whether a test's results can be generalized from an individual or group to the larger population. Compensatory grading is the practice of balancing out lower performance in one area or subject with higher performance in another. Noncompensatory grading does not permit such balancing, but requires a similar standard of achievement in each area or subject. A cut score is a predetermined number used to divide categories of data or results from a test instrument. For example, a cut score can divide the categories of passing and failing scores. It can also divide the category of passing scores from a category of "honors" or "excellent" or "superior" scores.

Standard Deviation, Standard Score, and Scaled Score

Standard deviation measures variability within a set of numbers. In interpreting assessment results, it measures how much scores among a group of test-takers vary around the mean/average. For example, a bell curve shows a normal distribution of test scores: the high center represents the majority of scores closest to the mean, while the lower sides represent standard deviations above and below it. SD is calculated by obtaining the square root of the sum of deviations of each score

Copyright © Mometrix Media. You have been licensed one copy of this document for personal use only. Any other reproduction or redistribution is strictly prohibited. All rights reserved.
This content is provided for test preparation purposes only and does not imply an endorsement by Mometrix of any particular political, scientific, or religious point of view.

and the mean, and dividing this figure by the number of scores in the group. The standard score, or z score, represents the amount whereby an individual score deviates from the mean, measured in SDs. For example, a common SD unit for IQ tests is 15 where the mean is 100. A scaled score is obtained by converting a group of test scores to a scale/distribution with a designated mean and SD. For example, the US Medical Licensing Examination (USMLE) has a mean of 200 and a SD of 20.

Domain and the Item Response Theory

In educational assessment, the term "domain" is the identified scope of expected learning to be assessed. Tests typically present students with samples of assessment tasks. The results of these tests are then interpreted to generalize the performance on the full range of possible assessment tasks that would measure the domain of intended learning. Item Response Theory (IRT) posits that performance on a test item is attributed to three influences: the item itself; the test-taker; and the interaction between the two. In education, when large groups of test-takers are given many test items to produce large data sets, raters can use formulae to separate influences on test items from the test-takers' true ability, skills, or knowledge. However, the kind of assessment that is normally conducted within a given educational program does not afford enough data to calculate parameters according to Item Response Theory that would be stable enough to be meaningful.

Mean, Median, and Mode

The mean is the average of a group of numbers, e.g., scores within a group of students taking the same test. Among six students, if one scores 50%; one 60%; one 70%; one 80%; one 90%; and one 100%, the sum of scores = 450; divided by 6 (students/scores) yields an average/mean of 75%. The median is the center-most score in a group. For example, if the range of student scores on a test is 65%, 75%, 80%, 85%, and 95%, then 80% = the middle/median. When there is an even number of scores, the median is the average of the two most central scores. For example, with four scores of 50%, 60%, 70%, and 80%, 60% and 70% are averaged for a median of 65%. The mode is the most frequent score in a set. If in a group of students, one scored 100% on a test; one, 95%; two, 90%; three, 85%; four, 80%; three, 75%; two, 70%; and one, 65%, the mode = 80%.

Positive Skew, Negative Skew, and Normal Distribution

When the majority of a group of numbers, such as test scores, is concentrated toward the high end of the range/distribution with the minority "tail" of scores near the low end, this group of numbers is said to be positively skewed. When the majority of scores is bunched near the lower end of the distribution, with a minority "tail" near the higher end, the set of scores is negatively skewed. A normal curve is called a bell curve because it resembles the shape of a bell, with the largest number of scores collected around the center mean or average score and the numbers of scores descending as they move away from the center and mean. Parametric statistics assume a normal distribution. However, in typical educational assessments, the data obtained as scores on testing instruments are not usually found to be distributed normally.

SEM and Standard Error of the Mean

If an individual student took a lot of tests that were similar in size or length (i.e., the number of items on each test), the assessors can estimate how much that student's scores will vary. This estimate is called the Standard Error of Measurement (SEM). The SEM is calculated using the reliability coefficient that is established for a given test and the Standard Deviation (SD) that has been established for the group of scores that the student achieved. When a group of students takes a test, the assessors can estimate how much the mean or average score of that group would vary if they selected many samples with the same sizes and then calculated the means or averages of their scores. This estimate of variance around the mean of a group's test scores is called the Standard Error of the Mean.

Copyright © Mometrix Media. You have been licensed one copy of this document for personal use only. Any other reproduction or redistribution is strictly prohibited. All rights reserved.
This content is provided for test preparation purposes only and does not imply an endorsement by Mometrix of any particular political, scientific, or religious point of view.

Confidence Interval

Statisticians use the Confidence Interval to express the range wherein a "true" or "real" score is situated. The purpose is to acknowledge and address the fact that the measurement of a student's performance contains "noise," i.e., interfering/confounding variables that influence the measure of pure ability/achievement, akin to static in a radio, phone, or other sound signal. Giving a Confidence Interval shows the probability that a student's true score is within the range defined by that interval. For example, a student might take a test and receive a score of 80%. If that student took several other, similar tests, most likely the student's scores would not all be exactly 80%; they would be similar, but vary. The assessors might give a Confidence Interval of + 2 Standard Deviations, 95% of the time. Computing Confidence Intervals does not use Standard Scores (z scores), but literal scores to show the upper and lower limits of the range of likely scores.

Cut Score

Educators use a cut score to determine which scores are passing and which are failing. They set a particular number as the cut score; all scores above it are passing and all scores below the cut score are failing. Using methods developed for multiple-choice tests allows them to adjust for various factors, e.g., the difficulty of a certain test or assessing student population with special needs, rather than arbitrarily assigning the same cut score to all tests. One such method for establishing a cut score is the Nedelsky method: the assessor(s) identify a "borderline" group of students, i.e., those who do not always pass or fail, but tend to score on the borderline of passing/failing. The assessor(s) estimate how many of these "borderline" students will probably answer a given test item correctly. A common number for this group is 10 students. The sum of the percentages of students estimated to respond correctly to each test item is rounded to an integer, yielding the cut score.

Angoff Method for Determining a Pass/Fail Cut Score

To determine which scores on a given test are passing or failing, educators can use several established methods. In the Angoff method, one or more assessors select a group of "borderline" students (i.e., those not always passing or failing but with equal chances of either) and estimate which choice(s) in a multiple-choice test item these students could eliminate as an incorrect answer and what percent of the choices left these students would guess as correct. For example, if they might eliminate one choice of five as wrong, their probability of guessing the right choice from the four choices left is 25% (1/4). The assessors add up the percentages for all of the test items and round the sum to an integer, which would be the cut score for that test. In the modified Angoff procedure, the assessors also estimate how many of the students would fail the test, and if they deem it necessary, they modify their estimations to produce a number of failures they find more reasonable.

Ebel Method for Determining a Pass/Fail Cut Score

Rather than arbitrarily setting the same pass/fail cut score for all tests, several methods exist for determining an appropriate cut score for a particular instrument. The Ebel method considers the importance and difficulty level of each test item in establishing a cut score for a test. First the testers divide all test items into six categories: High, Medium, and Low importance; and High, Medium, and Low difficulty. Then, after selecting a group of "borderline" students who do not always pass or fail tests but are about equally likely to do either, they estimate how many of these students would probably get each item correct in each of these six categories. They add up their estimated percentages for each test item and round the sum to an integer, which is the cut score. The assessors can also then modify their estimations based on data they may obtain from a student class or group's actual test results.

Copyright © Mometrix Media. You have been licensed one copy of this document for personal use only. Any other reproduction or redistribution is strictly prohibited. All rights reserved.
This content is provided for test preparation purposes only and does not imply an endorsement by Mometrix of any particular political, scientific, or religious point of view.

HOFSTEE METHOD TO DETERMINE PASS/FAIL CUT SCORES

Several methods have been developed to set a cut score, the score above which all scores are passing and below which all scores are failing, for a particular test with a multiple-choice format. The Hofstee method is also called the compromise method. It addresses the difference between norm-referenced and criterion-referenced tests, i.e., tests that compare individual student scores to the average scores of a normative sample of students found representative of the larger population versus tests that compare student scores to a pre-established criterion of achievement. Educators estimate an acceptable number of students who would fail the test and the largest number of test items a student who fails the test would answer correctly. They then plot the answers to this number of items plus two more on the cumulative score distribution. This allows them to determine how many items students could miss and how many failed test items would affect the number of students who could fail.

NORM-REFERENCED TESTS AND CRITERION-REFERENCED TESTS

In reference to testing large groups, like the entire student body of a school, district, or state, the high-stakes standardized tests given are typically norm-referenced tests; that is, they compare students' scores to a normative sample of students deemed representative of the general population. Criterion-referenced tests may or may not be standardized and compare student scores to a predetermined set of criteria for acceptable performance. In the context of educational programs, norm-referenced tests seek to determine the highest or lowest achievement rather than the absolute score achieved. For example, educators might determine the 10 highest student scores on a certain test to reinforce with "best in group" awards. In this context, measures of mastery learning are examples of criterion-referenced or domain-referenced testing. Educators establish a minimum performance level score that equates to passing. Student scores are compared against this score, so the students in a given class could all pass or all fail the test.

FORMATIVE ASSESSMENTS VERSUS SUMMATIVE ASSESSMENTS

Formative assessments are given during a lesson, unit, course, or program. Their purpose is to give the teachers and students an idea of how well each student is learning what the teacher has planned and expected for them to learn. The teacher uses the results of formative assessments to explain to each student his/her strengths and weaknesses, and how s/he can build on the strengths and improve the weaknesses, and to report student progress to parents, administrators, and others. Summative assessments are given after a lesson, unit, course, or program has been completed. Their purpose is to determine whether the student has passed the segment of instruction. This determines whether they need to repeat the instruction or can move on to successive segments. Summative assessments apply to lessons or units within a class, to courses in a subject, to promotion from one grade level to the next, and to graduation.

ITEM ANALYSIS

Item analysis is often used to evaluate test items that use multiple-choice formats to show the quality of the test item and of the test overall. Item analysis has an implicit orientation of being norm-referenced rather than criterion- or domain-referenced. That is, it evaluates test items using performance within the group of test-takers rather than an externally preset criterion for expected achievement. Characteristics analyzed in test items include how many high-scoring students got an item correct; how many low-scoring students got the item correct; the test item's discrimination index for separating high- and low-scoring test-takers; the test item's difficulty index; how many test-takers chose each of the answer choices on each test item; the quality of the correct answer choices; and the reliability of the test, i.e., how consistent its results are across separate administrations to the same test-takers.

Copyright © Mometrix Media. You have been licensed one copy of this document for personal use only. Any other reproduction or redistribution is strictly prohibited. All rights reserved.
This content is provided for test preparation purposes only and does not imply an endorsement by Mometrix of any particular political, scientific, or religious point of view.

DISCRIMINATION INDEX AND DIFFICULTY INDEX

The discrimination index is a measure of how well a specific test item can separate students who generally score high on the test from students who generally score low on it. Educators obtain a point biserial correlation between high total scores and low total scores with correct or incorrect item responses. Typically, they use total test scores to select the top 27% and bottom 27% of test-takers to magnify the variation between high and low test performance. When analyzing standardized, norm-referenced tests, the preferred discrimination index is .50. The difficulty index is a simple measure of how difficult a test item is considered. It is obtained by calculating the percentage of all students taking a test who answered a certain test item correctly.

SENSITIVITY AND SPECIFICITY AND THE KR20 FORMULA

Sensitivity refers to how well a test identifies every member of a defined group. The more sensitive a test is, the more likely it can include some individuals who should not be in that group. Specificity refers to how well a test identifies only those members of a defined group. The more specific a test is, the more likely it will omit some individuals who should be included in that group. Among many KR formulas used to estimate statistically a test's reliability or consistency, the KR20 is one that assumes that the relative difficulty of items on a test, and the correlations among those items, are basically equal. The KR20 formula deducts the variances of all individual test items from the total test's variance, which produces an estimate of the test's internal consistency reliability. When a test has items of dissimilar difficulty, the Horst's modification can be used to correct for this by estimating the maximal variance possible within a given range of item difficulties for that test.

MODIFIED ASSESSMENTS OF STUDENTS WITH SPECIAL NEEDS ON STANDARDIZED TESTS

Exclusive of actual test items, in some states the test administration instructions may be clarified or simplified. Other than item responses, students may be allowed to highlight or make other marks in their test booklets. Students may be tested in small groups rather than whole class settings. Test administrators may give students additional time within the testing day to complete a test. Individual students may be tested separately with direct examiner supervision. Students with visual impairments may use visual magnifiers for test text, and hearing-impaired students may use audio amplification. Individual study carrels/enclosures may be used as noise buffers for hearing-impaired or distractible students. Special lighting, acoustics, special furniture, or adaptive furnishings may be allowed. Masking or colored overlays may be used to sustain student visual attention. American Sign Language (ASL) or Manually Coded English (MCE) may also be used to give test instructions (but not test items) to deaf, hard-of-hearing, or nonverbal students.

Some states allow students to mark their test responses in their test booklets, and then the school personnel transfer these onto the standardized answer form used by other students to be electronically scored. For students with vision, hearing, manual, or motor impairments, they may dictate their responses to multiple-choice test items aloud or in American Sign Language (ASL) or Manually Coded English (MCE) to a designed scribe who writes, types, or fills in bubbles, circles choices, or otherwise marks the student's answers on a form. For essay questions, some students may be permitted to use word processing software programs, with the spell-check and grammar-check features disabled. Other students may be allowed to dictate their essay answers orally to a voice recorder or scribe, or manually in sign language to an interpreter/scribe, or using speech-to-text computer software. In these cases, students supply all writing conventions of spelling and grammar in their dictation. Assistive devices that allow independent student work may be used.

For blind or visually impaired students or those with visual processing deficits, testers may provide Braille transcriptions of the printed test; large-print versions of the test; or, if the student needs larger type than the fonts used in large-print versions, test items may be enlarged. Students who

Copyright © Mometrix Media. You have been licensed one copy of this document for personal use only. Any other reproduction or redistribution is strictly prohibited. All rights reserved.
This content is provided for test preparation purposes only and does not imply an endorsement by Mometrix of any particular political, scientific, or religious point of view.

require additional time and/or shorter testing durations (e.g., those with cognitive impairments, attention deficits, or behavior disorders) may be allowed to take a test normally administered in one sitting over more than one day and/or take supervised breaks during one test section. Medication effects and fluctuating attention and/or performance levels can be addressed by administering tests at the optimal time of day for the student. Examiners may test some students in homes or hospitals. Test items and answer choices may be presented in sign language, audio recordings, or read aloud. On math and science tests, like in fifth grade, some students may be allowed to use calculators and/or concrete math manipulatives.

Modified Assessment Procedures for ELL or ESL Students

Students whose native language is not English are allowed some variations by the US states to participate in standardized testing in the English language on a more equable footing with native English speakers. For example, they may hear the printed test instructions translated into their native language and read aloud. They may be allowed to ask questions in their native language to clarify test instructions. ESL/ELL students may be granted additional, supervised breaks during a testing day or test portion, providing they complete the portion within the testing day. (Standardized tests typically display a "STOP" sign to indicate the ends of test portions.) Students learning English may be allowed to take tests separately in groups with other ELL/ESL students, under supervision by school personnel cleared for test security, particularly if their regular instruction and/or testing have included similar flexibility. ELL/ESL students taking math and science tests may be permitted access to word lists or glossaries translated from English to their native language, excluding formulae or definitions.

General Adaptions to Assessments for Special-Needs Students

General testing adaptations include using these oral directions interchangeably: "Find," "Show me," "Point to," and "Give me." Testers should place stimulus cards and manipulatives however the student is best able to perceive these. Concrete materials should be set on surfaces with boundary edges so they cannot roll away or fall down when students use them. Testers should arrange the test environment to eliminate or reduce distractions for students more susceptible to these. For visually impaired students, testers may enlarge stimulus cards as needed. They may replace visual stimuli with Braille, beeping objects or other auditory stimuli, or textured materials if the student is accustomed to using these regularly. Testing teachers can cut out the outlines of shapes or figures from stimulus cards. They may substitute spoken cues like "Tell me" instead of "Show me." As necessary, they may describe the content of pictorial stimuli. They should let students handle concrete objects as is needed. Students who wear corrective glasses should always wear these during assessments.

Teachers can allow students to use augmentative communication devices for receiving and responding to test stimuli. For students who use American Sign Language (ASL) or manually coded English, teachers should use these languages or have an interpreter use them instead of spoken instructions or stimuli whenever appropriate. Nonverbal students should be allowed to give test responses using vocalizations, gestures, or movements instead of speech. Some students may draw pictures instead of writing. (This can also apply to students with dyslexia.) As is appropriate, teachers may accept eye gazes as responses instead of speech or gesture. Students who wear hearing aids must wear them during assessments; teachers should check that they work first. Students with sensorimotor impairments should be given longer times to initiate responses. Teachers should accept changes in facial expressions or muscle tone as observed behaviors. Teachers should stabilize and position students to afford the most controlled possible motions. Teachers should also let students direct others to perform physical tasks.

Copyright © Mometrix Media. You have been licensed one copy of this document for personal use only. Any other reproduction or redistribution is strictly prohibited. All rights reserved.
This content is provided for test preparation purposes only and does not imply an endorsement by Mometrix of any particular political, scientific, or religious point of view.

Technological Development of Portfolio Assessments

Just as physical portfolios show a student's work and creative products accumulated over time, ePortfolios store documents and photos of products and can be shared with others; but given the advent of social networks, they benefit from additional advantages of immediate communication and reinforcement. Digital archives can portray a student's life, from birth through early childhood family learning via scrapbooks, and through formal schooling and into employment and professional development. In portfolios, key processes include collecting products for the digital archive; selecting those demonstrating certain standards or goals by creating hyperlinks for others, which leads to reflecting or metacognition, helping the student construct meaning from the works s/he selected, aided by new storytelling models generated by technology; directing or goal-setting; presenting ePortfolios; and getting feedback on them. Social networking includes processes of connecting with others; listening to or reading posts; responding by commenting on posts; and sharing via linking or tagging. Key processes technology enables include archiving; linking and thinking; digital storytelling; collaborating; and publishing.

Students can be internally motivated (self-directed by inner goals) or externally motivated by outer rewards. The ePortfolios enabled by technology can support students' internal motivation and autonomy by establishing online environments wherein others feel good about participating, keeping systems relatively open, and giving users freedom to participate. Social networks support student autonomy by giving them choices and voices in the content they post and view; opportunities to share and give feedback; and far greater immediacy in all of their interactions. Students can experience academic and personal mastery through social networking, which affords the motivational factors of what Csikszentmihályi called "flow" (energized, positive, task-aligned, spontaneous, single-minded, focused, immersed, joyful, deep, and total engagement in an activity); the ability to showcase their achievements; and the benefits of enhanced self-insight and self-awareness. Via choice and personalization, students find their passions and voices. Constructing ePortfolios also helps students develop senses of purpose by engaging in something beyond themselves, understanding the relevance of what they learn, and seeing the "big picture."

Screening to Identify Students Who Need Special Education Services

Screening is the important first step of the assessment process mandated by federal laws. All newborns should be screened for developmental disabilities, and children should continue to be screened through early childhood, preschool, and school years. While more obvious disabilities like spina bifida, cerebral palsy, Down syndrome, autism, multiple disabilities, or severe sensory impairment are detected early, others like learning disabilities, ADHD, and some behavior disorders often go unidentified until school. Public schools typically conduct periodic screenings of large student groups from grades K–3. Very low standardized achievement test scores can lead to referral for formal evaluation—only with written parental consent—to identify possible disabilities. Also, students' parents, teachers, and other school staff may identify students with suspected disabilities, as when they evidence behavioral or academic difficulties in classrooms. Some students are not identified with disabilities until higher grades, due to ineffective screening, referral, assessment, and/or identification procedures; to disabilities acquired later through injury, illness, etc.; or to problems not apparent until school demands surpass student coping skills.

Problems and Solutions with School-Based Screening

While school screenings are vital and the process of identifying students with disabilities has a basic structure, there are no uniform or standardized sets of checklists, procedures, or testing instruments to identify disabilities in most students. The kinds of referral processes and tests utilized vary, both across and within states. According to educational experts, two main problems with screening procedures are over-identification and under-identification of disabilities. Research

Copyright © Mometrix Media. You have been licensed one copy of this document for personal use only. Any other reproduction or redistribution is strictly prohibited. All rights reserved.
This content is provided for test preparation purposes only and does not imply an endorsement by Mometrix of any particular political, scientific, or religious point of view.

studies have shown that students have been over-identified with learning disabilities, while students with behavior disorders are under-identified, especially compliant students who are not aggressive or disruptive but have problems like social isolation, depression, or school phobia. Educators have been improving screening procedures to resolve these problems. For example, Walker et al (1990) created the Systematic Screening for Behavioral Disorders with three steps: first, teachers rank students according to designated criteria; then select the three highest ranked students and complete checklists to quantify their observations about them; and school psychologists/counselors observe identified students prior to any formal evaluation referrals.

Prereferral Interventions

Prereferral interventions are a frequent practice intended to better the process of identifying students with disabilities by decreasing referrals to special education services and give regular education teachers more assistance and advice. Rather than first referring a student for evaluation to diagnose a possible disability, teachers initially try to address behavior or learning problems in the classroom through modifications. Only if modifications are found inadequate to the student's difficulties, and the teacher believes special services may be required, does s/he initiate the referral process. Most states in the US require or recommend prereferral intervention in some form. One approach uses Teacher Assistance Teams (TATs). TATs usually comprise four members: the referring teacher and three other teachers. These teams provide teachers with a forum to meet, discuss, and brainstorm ideas to instruct students and/or manage them. Another approach is collaborative consultation. Specialists like speech-language pathologists work directly with referring teachers in planning, implementing, and evaluating instruction for students identified in regular education classrooms.

Identification through Child Find, Referral, or Request for Evaluation

Under the federal IDEA law, each US state is held responsible for locating, identifying, and evaluating all children in that state as having disabilities and in need of special education and related services. To carry out this mandate, the states engage in Child Find processes. This is one way that children are identified with disabilities. The state's Child Find system may ask a child's parents for permission to evaluate the child, or parents can contact the Child Find system themselves and request evaluation of their child. Another way children are identified is by referral. A teacher or other school professional suspecting a student might have a disability may request, in writing or orally, the student's evaluation. Parents must give consent before the evaluation can be made. The law also stipulates that a requested evaluation be within a reasonable time after receiving parental consent. Parents who suspect disability in their child may also request that the school evaluate the child.

Evaluation and Eligibility Determination

After screenings and prereferral interventions have been completed and a student is referred for formal evaluation or evaluation is requested, professionals must evaluate all developmental/learning areas related to the disability suspected. Test results are applied to decisions regarding eligibility for special education and related services, and an appropriate educational program. If parents disagree with evaluation results, they have the right under the IDEA to arrange an Independent Educational Evaluation (IEE) and to request payment for this evaluation by the school system. Once evaluation results have been collected and reported, parents meet with teachers and other qualified professionals to review them. They decide together whether the student meets the IDEA definition of a "child with a disability." Parents are entitled under the law to request a hearing challenging the eligibility decision if they disagree. If the child is found eligible for special education and related services, an IEP team must meet within 30 calendar days of eligibility determination to write an IEP.

Copyright © Mometrix Media. You have been licensed one copy of this document for personal use only. Any other reproduction or redistribution is strictly prohibited. All rights reserved.
This content is provided for test preparation purposes only and does not imply an endorsement by Mometrix of any particular political, scientific, or religious point of view.

First IEP Meeting After Eligibility is Determined

After a student is determined eligible for special education and related services according to the IDEA, the school must schedule the first meeting to write an Individualized Education Program (IEP) for the student. The IDEA mandates that ALL students that receive special education and related services must have an IEP written for them. By this law, the school system must contact the parents and all others who are to participate in the IEP process. They must inform the parents early enough to ensure they are able to arrange to attend the meeting. They must schedule the meeting at a place and time with which the parents and the school agree. They must inform the parents of the purpose of this meeting and its location, date, and time. They must also inform the parents who else will be attending the meeting. The school staff is also to inform the parents that they may invite any other people to the IEP meeting who have special expertise or knowledge about their child.

In the first IEP meeting for a student, the IEP team includes the student, the parents, the student's teacher(s), specialists, other school personnel who interact with the student; outside consultants if invited; and any others with knowledge about the student, invited by the parents. If a group other than this IEP team decides placement for the student, the parents must also be included in that group. Parents must give consent before initial provision of special education and related services. With this consent, services must commence as soon as possible following the first IEP meeting. When parents disagree with the content of the IEP and/or their child's placement, they can discuss this with other IEP team members and work toward solutions. If the parents still disagree, they may request mediation or the school can offer mediation services. Parents also have the right to file complaints with the state education agency and to request a due process hearing. Mediation must be made available at this hearing.

IEP Implementation

Once the IEP team has met and developed an IEP for a student and the parents agree with it, the school must give them a copy of the IEP. Each teacher and service provider working with the student can access the student's IEP and must know his/her specific duties in implementing the IEP. The school must ensure that the IEP is implemented as it is written, including providing all accommodations, modifications, and supports to the student as specified in the IEP document. As outlined in the IEP, the school must measure the student's progress toward yearly IEP goals. The school regularly informs the parents of their child's progress and whether it is sufficient for meeting the annual goals. Progress reports must be provided at least as frequently as those reporting nondisabled students' progress. IEPs are reviewed at least annually—more if the parents or the school request it. The IEP is revised if needed. Parents must be invited to review meetings, can suggest changes, and agree/disagree with IEP goals and/or placement.

Legal Requirements for Reevaluation in IEP Process

All students receiving special education and related services are required by law to have an Individualized Education Plan (IEP). It is developed by the IEP team, which includes the student, parents, teachers, other school employees, other professionals, and any others invited by parents or schools who have contributions relevant to the student and his/her education. The student has received a formal evaluation to determine eligibility. The IEP is reviewed at least annually or more often if the school or parents request it and is revised as needed. Additionally, the student must be reevaluated at least every three years. Educators often call such reevaluation a "triennial." Reevaluation is made to determine whether the student still meets the IDEA definition of a "child with a disability" or not, and to reexamine the educational needs of the student. The three-year interval is a minimum, though: if circumstances indicate it, and/or if the parents or teachers request a new evaluation, the student must be reevaluated sooner than after three years.

Copyright © Mometrix Media. You have been licensed one copy of this document for personal use only. Any other reproduction or redistribution is strictly prohibited. All rights reserved.
This content is provided for test preparation purposes only and does not imply an endorsement by Mometrix of any particular political, scientific, or religious point of view.

Legally Required Information in IEP

Current Performance, Annual Goals, and Special Education and Related Services

The IDEA requires the IEP to state the student's "present levels of educational performance," i.e. the student's current progress in school. Results of evaluations made to determine eligibility for special services; classroom tests and in-class and homework assignments; and observations contributed by parents, teachers, related service providers, and other school personnel provide the information for the statement of the student's current school performance. This statement includes the impacts of the student's disability on his/her progress and engagement in the school's general education curriculum. Annual goals are those the student can reasonably attain within a school year. These are subdivided into short-term objectives, or benchmarks. Goals can be academic, behavioral, social, or physical. Goals must be measurable to show if the student has met them. The IEP must name all special education and related services to be provided to or on behalf of the student, including supplementary services and aids; changes to the program; and training, professional development, or other provisions supporting school staff in providing services to the student.

Student's Participation with Nondisabled Students, Participation in Statewide and District-Wide Testing; and Dates and Locations of Services

All students identified with disabilities and eligible for special education and related services must have IEPs (Individualized Education Programs). The IEP must include an explanation of the degree, if any, to which the student will NOT be participating with nondisabled students in regular classrooms and other school activities. Regarding statewide and district-wide standardized achievement tests regularly given by school systems to students at certain age or grade levels, the IEP must identify which modifications in test administration the student will need. Moreover, if any such test is deemed inappropriate for a particular student, the student's IEP must explain why and state what alternative testing will be substituted. The student's IEP must also state when the student's special education and related services will start, how often services will be provided, in what locations services will be given, and the duration of the services.

Transition Services, Student's Reaching the Age of Majority, and Progress Measurement

While a student reaches the age of 14—or sooner when applicable—the student's IEP must include in its pertinent sections which courses the student must take to attain his/her postschool goals. Every IEP following this must also contain a statement of the student's needs in transition services. Transition may be to postsecondary education; job training; and/or community living. When the student is 16 years old—or before if appropriate—the IEP must define which transition services the student will need as preparation for exiting the current school program/system. At least one year before the student reaches the age of majority, his/her IEP must state the student has been informed of any rights that will transfer from parents/caregivers to him/her. This only applies in states where rights are transferred when minor children reach majority age. Law requires the IEP to state how the school will measure the student's educational progress and how it will inform the student's parents of their child's progress.

Additional Content School Systems and States May Include in IEPs

While the IDEA federally mandates certain content in students' IEPs, individual states and school systems have much flexibility regarding what other information they require. Since federal law dictates that school districts document their compliance with federal requirements, some states and school systems choose to add information in their students' IEPs that serves to document their compliance with both federal and state laws. In general, some examples of additional elements IEPs can contain that document this compliance include: documentation that the school held the

Copyright © Mometrix Media. You have been licensed one copy of this document for personal use only. Any other reproduction or redistribution is strictly prohibited. All rights reserved.
This content is provided for test preparation purposes only and does not imply an endorsement by Mometrix of any particular political, scientific, or religious point of view.

meeting(s) for writing, reviewing, and revising when necessary the student's IEP on a timely basis; documentation that the school furnished the student's parents with a copy of their legally mandated procedural safeguards and rights; documentation that the school has placed the student in the least restrictive environment possible where s/he can experience adequate learning and progress; and documentation that the school received parental consent to provide their child with evaluations, special education, and related services.

KEY MEMBERS OF THE IEP TEAM

Members of a student's IEP team are not limited to, but include: the student; the parents; the special education teacher(s); specialist(s) or other service provider(s); the regular education teacher(s); someone able to interpret evaluation results; a representative of the school system; a representative of a transition services agency; and others having special expertise/knowledge about the student. (Sometimes an individual member fulfills more than one of these functions.) Parents are important team members for knowledge of their child, including his/her strengths and needs and their ideas about how to improve his/her education. Parents can contribute insights about their child's learning style and processes, what academic and life areas are of particular interest to their child, and other things only parents know about their children. Parents can consider other team members' recommendations about areas to focus on in school and can share their own suggestions. Additionally, parents can report to the school whether their child is applying skills s/he has learned in school, at home, and in other settings outside school.

The IEP team member who can interpret evaluation results can not only explain to other members what test results signify, e.g., the type of disability and deficit areas, but moreover how to design instruction appropriate to the student and characteristics identified by evaluation results. Skillfully interpreting test results informs the team how the student is currently faring in school and helps them pinpoint areas of particular student needs. This member's role is not only understanding and explaining test results, but furthermore explaining the instructional implications of those results and helping plan accordingly suitable instruction. The school system representative contributes extensive knowledge about teaching students with disabilities and about the special education services available in the school system. This member can discuss the school resources the student and educators will need. It is also important for this individual to have the authority for committing school system resources, and the ability for assuring all services specified in the IEP are actually provided to the student and staff.

If a special education student participates in regular education at all (which is increasingly the case these days), at least one of the student's regular education teachers must be included in the IEP team. This teacher can inform other team members about the regular classroom's general curriculum, and also what kinds of services, changes in the educational program, and/or aids would help the student to learn and succeed best. S/he can also suggest strategies for managing classroom behavior if this is an issue. The regular education teacher can also talk with the rest of the team about which supports the school staff will need to help the student progress toward annual IEP goals, engage in regular curriculum and succeed in it, participate in extracurricular activities, and be included in instruction with both nondisabled and disabled peers. Such school staff supports can include additional training, professional development, etc., not only for teachers but also administrators, cafeteria staff, bus drivers, and all others providing services to students with disabilities..

Informed by her/his training and experience in special education, the special education teacher contributes to the IEP team by discussing various topics. These include how to make adaptations and modifications to the general education curriculum that will enable the student to learn in the

Copyright © Mometrix Media. You have been licensed one copy of this document for personal use only. Any other reproduction or redistribution is strictly prohibited. All rights reserved.
This content is provided for test preparation purposes only and does not imply an endorsement by Mometrix of any particular political, scientific, or religious point of view.

regular education setting; which supplementary services and aids the student is likely to require for succeeding in regular classrooms and other places; techniques for modification of assessments that enables the student to better demonstrate what s/he has learned; and additional elements of individualizing the instruction according to the unique needs of the student. Special educators not only help write IEPs; they are also responsible for working with students to implement them. They may do this in special education classes or resource rooms; team-teach with regular education teachers; and collaborate with regular education teachers and other school personnel, contributing expertise to meet the student's individual needs.

Parents and/or school system employees can invite individuals to participate as members of a student's IEP team based on their especial expertise and/or knowledge about the student. For instance, parents may know a professional with specific expertise in the student's particular disability; an advocate who has a relationship with the student; or a vocational educator who has been working with the student on employment skills. Such individuals are able to discuss the student's individual strengths and needs. The school system may also invite individuals, like paraprofessionals or professionals specializing in related services, who can contribute special expertise and/or knowledge about the student. A significant aspect of IEP development is the related services a student often needs; therefore, professionals specializing in such related services are frequently members or participants in the IEP team. These professionals can include physical therapists; occupational therapists; adaptive physical education instructors; orientation and mobility specialists; ASL interpreters; speech-language pathologists; psychologists; and others.

Material Reviewed to Determine Special Education and Services Needed

To develop the IEP, the team reviews evaluation results including individual tests given to the student to determine eligibility for services; classroom tests the student has taken; and the observations of parents, teachers, related service providers, paraprofessionals, administrators, and others involved. These help the team characterize the "present levels of educational performance" of the student, i.e., how s/he is currently functioning in school. They develop yearly goals targeting areas of educational need identified through this information. Information specific to the student they discuss includes the student's strongest assets; recent evaluation and/or re-evaluation results; parents' ideas to improve the student's education; and the student's performance on district-wide and statewide standardized examinations. The team's discussion of what the student needs should be guided by how they can help the student progress toward meeting yearly goals; engage in the general education curriculum and make progress in it; be included in participation and education with other students, both with and without disabilities; and participate in nonacademic and extracurricular activities.

Legal Requirements Regarding a Student's Placement

Once an IEP team has developed and written a student's IEP, where this program will be implemented—i.e., the student's placement—must also be decided. In some US states, the IEP team is also the group that makes placement decisions. In others, a different group may decide student placements. However, in every instance the parents have the legal right to participate as members of the group deciding placement. Placement decisions must abide by the IDEA's requirements for the Least Restrictive Environment (LRE): students with disabilities must be educated together with students without disabilities to the maximum degree possible and fitting. In addition, the IDEA specifies that students with disabilities may only be removed from the regular school setting—to special classes or separate schools—if the severity and/or nature of the student's disability makes education in regular classes, including the use of supplementary services and aids, impossible to attain with satisfactory results.

Copyright © Mometrix Media. You have been licensed one copy of this document for personal use only. Any other reproduction or redistribution is strictly prohibited. All rights reserved.
This content is provided for test preparation purposes only and does not imply an endorsement by Mometrix of any particular political, scientific, or religious point of view.

Integrating Affective, Social, and Life Skills into Academic Curricula

Many students with disabilities need special education and support to learn daily living skills. With proper instruction, they can obtain and keep meaningful jobs and live in the community; but without specialized instruction, they frequently lose jobs and/or home placements. Life skills include proper attire, grooming, and hygiene; acceptable table manners; financial decision-making; and utilizing transportation to employment. Instruction in financial skills is required by some states, including counting money and making change; managing bank accounts; keeping personal budgets and records; making personal financial decisions; spending and using credit responsibly; estimating and paying taxes; paying bills; and renting/leasing. Household management includes housekeeping; meal preparation; doing/hiring home maintenance/repair; and new appliance warranty registration. Personal care includes obtaining health care, eschewing substance abuse; recognizing common illnesses, knowing prevention and treatment; and nutrition, physical fitness, and weight maintenance. Safety awareness includes recognizing safety/hazard signs, rules, and procedures; unfamiliar sounds and/or smells; and knowing emergency evacuation procedures. Buying, storing, planning, preparing, and eating balanced, appropriate meals are included.

In addition to skills in dress, hygiene, other personal care, finance, household management, safety awareness, and food preparation, students with disabilities must also receive instruction, integrated into academic curricula in school, in how to purchase and care for clothing. They must be instructed in responsible citizenship, including knowing their own civil rights and responsibilities; obtaining legal aid; reporting crimes; for males, registering with Selective Service at age 18; knowing and obeying laws; knowing about federal, state, and local governments; and voting. Disabled students must also learn about community resources available; how to select and plan leisure activities, appreciate their importance, and participate in them; to plan vacation activities and social events; and practice music, arts, crafts, hobbies, and sports. Students must also be instructed in community navigation, including knowing right from left and front from back; safety and traffic rules; carpooling and other transportation; reading maps; and when applicable, learning to drive and obtaining a driver's license and automobile insurance. Special and regular educators, families, and peers provide instruction.

Special Student Factors

The law requires a number of "special factors" for the IEP team to consider as applicable with individual students. If a student's behavior impedes his/her and/or other students' learning, the team must consider effective, positive behavioral supports and intervention techniques to manage, control, or change the behavior. If the student has limited English-language proficiency, the team must consider the student's linguistic need relative to his/her IEP. If a student is blind or visually impaired, the team must provide Braille texts or instruction in Braille, or determine through evaluations the student does not need such instruction. In the latter case, the team must specify any other methods and/or devices the student needs and provide these. The team must consider any communication needs a student may have. For deaf or hard-of-hearing students, the team must consider their communication and linguistic needs, including opportunities for communicating directly with peers and staff in ASL or their other customary communication method(s). The team must also consider any student needs for assistive technology services and/or devices.

Different Program Placement and Integration into Placement

A student's IEP may be implemented in various placement settings according to the individual student's needs. Settings include placement in the regular education class, with supplementary services and aids the student needs; in a special class for all or part of the school day, with other students all also receiving special education and related services; in a special school dedicated to students needing special education and related services; in a hospital; in an institutional facility;

Copyright © Mometrix Media. You have been licensed one copy of this document for personal use only. Any other reproduction or redistribution is strictly prohibited. All rights reserved.
This content is provided for test preparation purposes only and does not imply an endorsement by Mometrix of any particular political, scientific, or religious point of view.

and other settings. To fulfill its legal requirements to make sure a student is placed appropriately, a school system can take various actions. For example, it may furnish the student with a suitable program as part of the school system. Or it may contract with an outside agency that can provide the student with an applicable program. Or it may make some other arrangements and/or make use of other mechanisms available to pay for or otherwise provide the student a program appropriate and consistent with the terms of the IDEA.

Prioritizing Areas of the General Education Curriculum for Students with Disabilities

The IDEA and ESEA Acts require all students' access to general education curriculum. Educators can help disabled students by connecting academic content to real-life activities. Achievement standards include the same academic content, but utilize alternate performance indicators still fitting content standards for reading and math. While alternative assessment methods and definitions of achievement standards vary considerably across states, educators in all states must provide instruction effective in helping students with disabilities meet standards. Teachers in some states select which responses are assessed to document progress toward state standards—e.g., portfolio assessments; specific choice-making; sight words; task analyses; generalized responses, like requests; problem-solving; and self-initiation responses. Systematic prompting with feedback, reinforcement, correction, and fading is an instructional support method. In general education settings, systematic instruction to small mixed-ability groups; cooperative learning groups; trials embedded in general education lectures/lessons; observational learning; peer tutors; and self-instruction and problem-solving materials are options. Assistive technology aids symbol use, and can reduce behavior problems and increase social interaction. Special and general educator planning collaboration is vital.

Copyright © Mometrix Media. You have been licensed one copy of this document for personal use only. Any other reproduction or redistribution is strictly prohibited. All rights reserved.
This content is provided for test preparation purposes only and does not imply an endorsement by Mometrix of any particular political, scientific, or religious point of view.

Curriculum, Instruction, and Intervention

Impact of Teachers' Attitudes and Behaviors on Student Achievement Outcomes

Research studies show that when teachers establish supportive relationships with their students; communicate clearly and consistently enforce high expectations of their students academically and behaviorally; and deliver a high quality of pedagogy and instruction to their students, the students are more likely to develop attitudes and behaviors of engagement in their learning, and perceptions of their own academic competence. These student attitudes and behaviors are found in turn to augment student achievement in key academic areas like reading and math. Experts define students' engagement as how much inherent interest they demonstrate in school, and the quantity and quality of their participation in schoolwork. This engagement and participation include both attitudes, like positive values about learning, motivation, interest, enthusiasm, and pride in succeeding, and also behaviors like attention, effort, and persistence. Therefore, students who are engaged pursue activities in and out of classrooms that further learning and/or succeeding. Additionally, they demonstrate curiosity, desire for more knowledge, and emotionally positive responses to school and learning.

Expectations and Student Behavior

Researchers have found that teachers are often unprepared for problem behaviors from both nondisabled and disabled students in urban school settings. Some reasons for such problem behaviors include the higher proportions in urban school populations of students from lower socioeconomic levels; of students from families who do not speak English; and of students with special needs. Some researchers have experimented with elementary-level urban schools by introducing a "Good Behavior" game. Teachers were directed to identify acceptable and unacceptable behaviors clearly to their students. Then they were to observe the students during specified periods of time and count the numbers of unacceptable behaviors. The individual student or group of students receiving the smallest number of recorded unacceptable behaviors would win the game. The researchers found that using this technique both increased on-task behaviors and decreased disruptive behaviors in the students. This approach is considered to be generalizable to schools in nonurban settings.

Factors in School That Influence Students' Motivation to Learn

One factor that is found to increase students' motivation to learn is a sense of belonging in their school settings and a sense of having caring relationships. This includes the students' feeling that their families and friends support them and their education, and in school particularly, that their teachers are supportive. Individualizing and personalizing their instruction is one way that teachers accomplish this. Teachers also create caring, supportive social environments in school by demonstrating interest in their students' lives, inside and outside school. Students experiencing such positive interpersonal relationships are found to display more positive attitudes and values regarding school, and more satisfaction with it, and to attend school more, learn more, and report more academic engagement. Another factor is clearly defined, high, consistent, and realistically attainable teacher expectations of student performance. A third factor promoting students' cognitive engagement is teachers' use of active pedagogical strategies challenging students to tackle new ideas, explain their thinking, defend their decisions, and/or explore alternate methods and solutions, especially through peer collaboration.

Copyright © Mometrix Media. You have been licensed one copy of this document for personal use only. Any other reproduction or redistribution is strictly prohibited. All rights reserved.
This content is provided for test preparation purposes only and does not imply an endorsement by Mometrix of any particular political, scientific, or religious point of view.

Student Activities That Promote Student Engagement

Educational research has found that students are more likely to experience and demonstrate greater classroom engagement over the long term of their education when teachers assign them to such hands-on, authentic activities as constructing models; planning, implementing, completing, and reporting on projects; participating in role-play exercises; participating in debates on topics relevant to school subjects and activities; and planning and conducting experiments, making conclusions about them, and reporting their results to their classmates and teachers. Studies have also shown that teachers can make the lessons that they teach more relevant and meaningful to students when these lessons draw from and build upon the students' existing background knowledge, cultural backgrounds, and experiences in the real world and life. When the material that they study is personally interesting to students and related to their lives, they both learn more effectively and also enjoy the learning process more.

Establishing Rapport in Early Elementary Grades

Teachers report warm lighting helps create a cozy, "at-home" atmosphere. Many elementary teachers assign a theme for the school year, like bugs, birds, fish, or rocks. They display posters illustrating the theme, including catchphrases expressing their learning strategies; incorporate the theme in first-day handouts, student folders, and parent letters; devise activities around the theme, like reading books to the class about the theme and assigning student pairs/small groups to design an original bug. On first days, teachers assign activities enabling students to move around, become comfortable with the classroom, get acquainted with each other, work collaboratively, and think creatively. They use games—searching for all classmates' names in puzzles or physically finding each classmate and collecting their signatures. Teachers use "brainteasers" to engage students in creative problem-solving. They take inventories of student interests on first days. And they assign students artistic activities—like cutting out and illustrating paper "T-shirts" identifying their preferences, interests, future dreams, past experiences, and adjectives describing themselves.

Modeling to Teach Eye Contact, Vocal Tone, and Pronunciation

Many autistic students avoid eye contact, as do some cognitively impaired students and even nondisabled younger students. Often they do not understand its importance and have no practice using it. Some teachers with teaching assistants or aides find it helps to model through conversations with them: the teacher says to the assistant that s/he noticed how the assistant's eyes were looking right at a student's eyes when they were talking; that this showed the student the assistant was listening, and the assistant could see the student was also listening; and praises the assistant for "good eye contact." The assistant replies that good eye contact during conversation is good manners. The same technique can be used to describe appropriate vocal tones for conversations and correct pronunciation. The teacher can follow up by asking students to demonstrate good eye contact when greeting another student. They observe and provide prompts as needed. This is most effective when the teacher immediately rewards the interaction with verbal praise, plus applause from the class.

Successfully Relating to and Instructing High School Students

Experienced high school teachers find that classroom success centers on three crucial areas: establishing rapport with the students; setting the teacher's rules and expectations for the class; and having strategies to promote students' motivation to learn. While teacher education students and new teachers observing experienced teachers may feel they seem to do it by some kind of magic, the experienced teachers say that strategic planning is actually at the heart of establishing a rapport and developing good working relationships with their students. For example, a high school teacher can help to build rapport with a new class of students by presenting oneself as having a

Copyright © Mometrix Media. You have been licensed one copy of this document for personal use only. Any other reproduction or redistribution is strictly prohibited. All rights reserved.
This content is provided for test preparation purposes only and does not imply an endorsement by Mometrix of any particular political, scientific, or religious point of view.

"stern yet caring" (as one teacher puts it) presence; set class rules and conduct other activities together *with* the students rather than unilaterally, which helps to establish a classroom community; and communicating one's expectations to the students clearly on the very first day of school.

Engaging Disabled and Younger Students in Paying Attention to Directions

Some experienced teachers use techniques like rhythmic clapping and/or chanting to engage student attention. For example, the teacher demonstrates a loud, rhythmic hand clap and tells the students that when they hear the teacher do this, they should stop what they are doing and imitate the hand clap. The teacher tells the students the clap means s/he has something important to share with them and to copy clapping when the teacher's hands go down, and s/he will know they are done when they make eye contact ("I see you looking at my eyes"). Teachers can chant directions, like "If you hear me, put your hands on your shoulders....If you hear me, put your hands on your hips....If you me, put your hands on your tummy...." Teachers enhance students' attention by modulating their voices. For students who do not pay attention, teachers instruct them aloud to be sure their hands are empty and they are looking at the teacher's eyes. Teachers may need to wait for all students to focus.

Establishing Rapport with Sixth-Grade Students

One way a sixth-grade teacher can get acquainted with new students is to give them surveys about their interests and surveys of Gardner's Multiple Intelligences to get ideas of students' preferences, strengths, needs, and learning styles. To assess student writing abilities and styles, a pre-assessment can involve writing a letter to the teacher about themselves. The teacher gives no pre-instructions on the steps of writing to discern what they already know how to do independently. The teacher may use her/his district's model for assessing writing. As icebreakers, teachers can assign as homework writing and illustrating a "Me" page, guided by teacher-given questions. They can have each student create a poster using the letters in their first name, filling the page with large "bubble" letters, and filling each letter with information, photos, or drawings about themselves. Then the teacher can display these in the classroom, integrating technology by adding printed digital photos of students to their posters. They can have students create slide shows and revise them at the end of the school year to add what they have learned.

Class Rules for Disabled and Nondisabled High School Students

The high school teacher can first establish basic, vital "ground rules" based on what the teacher needs in the classroom. For example, students must arrive on time and be prepared; respect both classmates and classroom materials; and follow directions the first time the teacher gives them. After conveying these rules, the teacher can involve students in collaborating to create class rules. This helps build a class community. The teacher can integrate the opinions and viewpoints of students by asking them simple questions, like why they are there and what they need to achieve their goals. The teacher records student answers, incorporating these in expanding on the ground rules. Involving students gives them a sense of a democratic class community instead of a dictatorship and stimulates processes of critical thinking. Teachers should also give students lists of daily materials needed and examples of acceptable versus unacceptable work, and inform students how they will assess their work (rubrics, etc.). Teachers should communicate their expectations orally, in print/writing, and visually.

Motivating High School Students to Read

Some high school teachers experienced in teaching teens who struggle with reading meet such challenges by getting students excited about reading. They find books their students can relate to and enjoy, and they can begin the school year by reading these books aloud to students. Only after

Copyright © Mometrix Media. You have been licensed one copy of this document for personal use only. Any other reproduction or redistribution is strictly prohibited. All rights reserved.
This content is provided for test preparation purposes only and does not imply an endorsement by Mometrix of any particular political, scientific, or religious point of view.

they have stimulated student enjoyment and enthusiasm for reading do they assess students' current reading levels, using instruments like the Scholastic Reading Inventory. Teachers can use a Book Pass activity to help students become familiar with books in their class library and select books with topics interesting to them at suitable levels for independent reading. Small groups (like five each) designate one student timekeeper. Seated in circles, each group member previews the front and back of the book and begins reading that book. The timekeeper announces when 2 to 3 minutes elapse; students write down the book title, pages read, comments, and whether they would like reading it further. Students then pass the books to their right, repeating with another book. They finish with group sharing of individual book comments.

Safe, Supportive, and Positive Elementary Classroom and School Climate

Elementary school teachers realize that students will be more engaged in school and learning if it is fun and they are happy. Some teachers help students consolidate what they just learned and/or take a break from schoolwork with a group singing period in the classroom. A few weeks into the school year, once students have gotten to know each other and developed into a cohesive group, some teachers have them vote for an alliterative class name reflecting their interests, ambitions, and/or attitudes. The teacher calls them by this group name when they are lining up to leave the room and at other key moments to reinforce their feelings of belonging and ownership. To encourage and reinforce student responsibility, some elementary teachers assign a job to each student for the week, posting these on a chart on the wall, and all of the students take turns assuming different weekly job rotations.

Communicating Expectations of Students and Regular Routines

Some schools use an acronym like BEST, representing Be respectful, Enjoy learning, Stay safe, and Totally responsible, to help students remember these principles. Some teachers have students negotiate their classroom expectations, keeping them generally consistent with school expectations, and on reaching consensus, they display pictures and words on the walls reflecting these. They also discuss choices and how expectations keep everyone safe. They set routines, posting their daily schedule on the wall and discussing it. Some teachers institute weekly lessons involving behavioral tasks explicitly teaching behavioral expectations aligned with school values, and they post these on the wall. Some teachers use a token economy. For example, each student gets a smiley face on a chart for making good choices; upon accumulating 10, the student can select a prize, which the teacher reports schoolwide to record all recognition of positive behaviors. When students do not meet expectations, some teachers explicitly model and teach expected behavior, like teaching how to apologize sincerely for hitting/kicking, with the victim choosing whether to accept the apology.

Addressing and Preventing Bullying

In April 2013, the US Department of Justice arrived at a settlement agreement with the Metropolitan School District of Decatur Township, Indiana. This concluded a review of district practices and policies regarding bullying and harassment, prompted by 2011 reports of possible racial targeting at one school. The district arranged to collaborate with the federally funded Great Lakes Equity Center at Indiana University-Purdue University Indianapolis on actions against bullying for disability, race, national origin, color, gender, or religion and promoting safe, supportive learning environments for all students. Actions include creating a district-wide antiharassment task force to review and revise district harassment/bullying and disciplinary policy and procedures; creating a coherent process to receive, investigate, and monitor bullying/harassment complaints, and track repeating instances involving groups/individuals in special classes; and give students and staff at two district schools school climate assessments, training, and professional development. A Civil Rights Division spokesperson said these affirmative

Copyright © Mometrix Media. You have been licensed one copy of this document for personal use only. Any other reproduction or redistribution is strictly prohibited. All rights reserved.
This content is provided for test preparation purposes only and does not imply an endorsement by Mometrix of any particular political, scientific, or religious point of view.

steps provide statewide and nationwide examples. Nationwide work against school bullying also aligns with federal civil rights legislation.

Icebreakers to Use to Get Acquainted with High School Students

Experienced high school teachers find adolescents are primarily concerned with adjusting to the new setting and getting acquainted with new classmates, and teachers need to start the year by familiarizing themselves well with new students. To help both teacher and students get acquainted, teachers can use icebreaker activities. One involves "matching" index cards based on common interests of the school's student body. For example, teachers make card pairs like Bill Gates and Microsoft; Russell Simmons and Def Jam Records, etc. Each student gets one card and finds the student with a matching card. Then they interview each other. Teachers can suggest questions, like the last school they attended, their favorite book genre, pet peeves, favorite things, embarrassing incidents, hobbies, etc. Following interviews, each student presents information about his/her "match" to the class. Another activity groups and numbers students in fours; each student writes down adjectives describing themselves and alliterative with their names (e.g., "Shy Shannon" or "Bookish Brad"), and take turns introducing themselves and another student using these.

Integrating Technology to Motivate Learning

To prepare and motivate adolescents to learn right away, high school teachers can integrate technology, yet need no more than a video camera and books when they assign projects the first week of school. For example, the teacher can ask the students to choose a book they have recently read and/or is their favorite. The teacher can lead a class discussion about characteristics in TV commercials that make the viewer remember the commercials best, like musical jingles; vivid visual imagery; strong slogans or tag lines; or humorous/incongruous situations. The teacher creates a model for students with a sample commercial. The teacher can then have the students make their own commercials advertising their chosen books. Another example of a project is to assign students to make their autobiographies, using videos about five minutes long. The teacher can guide the students to incorporate details related to their early childhoods; pets, friends, their home lives; their hobbies, what things interest them most, and what their major goals in life are.

Promoting Parental Support for Children's Education

Some teachers implement a practice of using a communication book for each student. These books are sent back and forth between the school and the students' homes for the teacher and parents to write correspondence to one another. Before calling the roll every morning, the teacher checks the communication books for new entries. (This practice likely works best with smaller class sizes.) Some elementary school teachers also invite all students' parents to visit their classrooms in the morning to help by reading or telling stories to the children to get them settled down and ready for the day. Some elementary school teachers regularly send notes to parents with students. For example, one teacher noticed her young students became hungry at midmorning, and the class agreed to schedule a snack period. She sent parents notes asking them to send healthy snack foods, including a list of appropriate, easy-to-prepare snacks. This teacher reported their snack time soon ran smoothly, with children usually eating and doing schoolwork concurrently.

Physical Education for Disabled Students

Federal Laws

The IDEA and other federal legislation for students with disabilities mandate that these students be provided physical education. Federal law defines physical education as the development of physical and motor skills; fundamental motor skills and patterns like catching, throwing, walking, running, etc.; and skills in individual and group sports, including intramural and lifetime sports, and in dance

Copyright © Mometrix Media. You have been licensed one copy of this document for personal use only. Any other reproduction or redistribution is strictly prohibited. All rights reserved.
This content is provided for test preparation purposes only and does not imply an endorsement by Mometrix of any particular political, scientific, or religious point of view.

and aquatics. The IDEA mandates instruction in the least restrictive environment (LRE) possible. Regarding PE, this involves adaptations and/or modifications to curriculum and/or instruction as it does regarding academic education. In PE, adaptations/modifications assure each student's success in a safe environment. A student's IEP defines placement, which can include one or several options among the general physical education setting alone; this setting but with aid from teaching assistants or peers; a separate PE class setting with peers; a separate PE class setting with assistants; and/or settings with 1:1 student-instructor activities.

Potential Modifications to Games

To level the competition, PE teachers can modify activities. They can let special-needs students hit or kick instead of pitching a ball. In volleyball games, they can let students catch and throw the ball and/or let it bounce. Teachers can permit longer time periods equal to student ability for moving to a goal/base. When possible, they can schedule games inside the gym on smooth floors to facilitate movement instead of outdoors in a field. When modifying rules for disabled students, teachers can involve them in the decision-making process. Teachers can reduce distances by moving bases closer together; letting students get closer to the net/goal/target; and letting them serve from midcourt in volleyball/badminton/tennis. Teachers can provide more scoring opportunities by substituting four for three strikes/ten arrows for six/three for two foul shots/etc. They can assign disabled students to be pitchers/goalies/first basemen, or other positions requiring less mobility. Adaptive equipment they can provide includes bigger bats/racquets; bigger/lighter/softer balls; and bigger baskets/goals/bases.

Benefits of Inclusive Educational Programs

Educational research has found that both students with disabilities and their nondisabled peers obtain significant benefits from inclusive educational programs. For example, students with disabilities experience more stimulating learning environments via inclusion. They benefit from nondisabled role models of adaptive, communication, and social skills and behaviors. They have more opportunities for making new friends and sharing new experiences with them. They gain greater peer acceptance from being included, and they have a greater sense of membership in a regular class and in the school. Students without disabilities benefit by learning greater acceptance of individual differences among people. They learn to feel more comfort around students with various disabilities. They learn to help their disabled peers, which generalizes to learning to be more helpful to others. They gain leadership skills by providing examples, help, and guidance. And they gain greater self-esteem through modeling helpful leadership behaviors. Thus, inclusive education benefits all students.

Adapting the Physical Environment to Facilitate Learning

For students whose cognitive levels, attention spans, or other differences make large assignments intimidating, teachers can divide these into small, more achievable "chunks" so they are more willing to tackle them and experience some success daily. For students having difficulty taking notes from the blackboard, teachers can offer paper handouts/notes. Distractible students can be seated away from windows, noisy, high-traffic areas, and classmates who encourage chatting. Teachers must implement all adaptations in student IEPs, monitor their effectiveness, and discuss changes with the team if adaptations are not enabling best student performance. With students needing constant reminding of how to follow class practices, teachers can make an enlarged checklist of expectations for their daily assignments/routines and tape it to their binder/desktop, enabling more independent work tracking. Scheduling morning periods daily to check student homework and planners clarifies expectations and allows time to resolve problems and still have productive days. Assignments and assessments can use computers/scribes/time extensions/oral responses as alternatives for students with writing/printing difficulties.

Copyright © Mometrix Media. You have been licensed one copy of this document for personal use only. Any other reproduction or redistribution is strictly prohibited. All rights reserved.
This content is provided for test preparation purposes only and does not imply an endorsement by Mometrix of any particular political, scientific, or religious point of view.

Arranging Physical Space to Accommodate Students

Teachers must consider all learning community members' needs, including students, teachers, specialists, paraprofessionals, and volunteers. When community members change, last year's arrangement may not work. Teachers must also consider size and layout of their classroom/space, including attached equipment/furnishings, classroom location in the school, and instructional materials. Depending on curriculum and teaching philosophy and approach, teachers may want to arrange space for large and small groups, teams, cooperative learning groups, and individual instruction. If any student(s) use wheelchairs, teachers must consider accommodating their maneuvering in the room. They must consider preventing distractions for ADHD students. They may lower chalkboards, bulletin boards, and pencil sharpeners, and add bathroom grab bars for wheelchair students, and they may procure more electrical outlets for computers, language masters, and tape recorders for students with LDs or visual impairment. They may place carpet in areas for students needing to sit/lie on the floor periodically. Insurmountable obstacles may dictate extensive remodeling or relocation to different classrooms. Advance planning is hence necessary to allow budgeting and work without interrupting school-year instruction.

Teachers should allocate areas within their classroom for individualized teaching, and also small and large groups. The teacher and/or learning specialist might need a small-group instruction space. Teaching stations, learning centers, and areas for partner/pair work are good whenever possible. Teachers need to separate/designate noisy and quiet areas, and spaces free of distractions. According to educational research, horizontal and vertical paths must allow teachers to reach any student within eight steps. Wheelchairs require at least 36" to maneuver. Student coats and backpacks must be placed to avoid blocking traffic. Some experts suggest having students turn their desks so the lids open away from them, to keep them from accumulating unwanted/forgotten things inside. If a classroom faces the playground, a busy road, student cafeteria lines, and/or steady streams of traffic—especially since classroom relocation, even when available, can take extreme effort and a whole year—teachers can adapt existing spaces by putting curtains over windows, closing the door, and hanging visual displays from the ceiling that absorb sound.

Instructional Accommodations and Modifications

Accommodations are changes in HOW students learn and are assessed, while modifications are changes in WHAT students are expected to learn. Accommodations can involve teaching methods, materials, assignments, tests, the learning environment, scheduling, time demands, and special communications systems, and they need not change school learning goals. Modifications can involve partial program or course completion; lower than grade-level curriculum expectations; alternative curriculum goals; and alternate assessments. The IDEA mandates that schools give students with disabilities the chance to be included and progress in the general education curriculum, which can require accommodations and/or modifications to accomplish. The IDEA also requires all students receiving special education and related services to have IEPs Section 504 of the Rehabilitation Act that requires that schools provide accommodations to students with disabilities even if they do not have IEPs. The Americans with Disabilities Act (ADA) bans discrimination against the disabled. State laws follow the federal laws in allowing accommodations and modifications for students with disabilities.

Effective Use of Common Spaces

While teachers have little or no control over their school building's commonly shared spaces, they can instruct their students to work with these. For example, they can teach them the common courtesies of walking quietly on the right side of the hall, and of speaking quietly in the library and cafeteria, auditorium, or cafeteria. This will help students adjust to large spaces inside the building. Teachers can also instruct all students to allow sufficient space for students using wheelchairs to go

Copyright © Mometrix Media. You have been licensed one copy of this document for personal use only. Any other reproduction or redistribution is strictly prohibited. All rights reserved.
This content is provided for test preparation purposes only and does not imply an endorsement by Mometrix of any particular political, scientific, or religious point of view.

around corners and not to crowd wheelchairs. This not only helps the students in wheelchairs; it also prevents ambulatory students from being injured by coming too close to wheelchairs. Students in both special and general education programs must be taught to take special care in adhering to rules and guidelines on the playground and in the school gymnasium. Students make successful adaptations to school building spaces when they have learned how to navigate from one place to another, and how to behave in each school area.

Accommodations for Students with Difficulties with Self-Control

Some students with disabilities can require alterations in the learning environment to assist them in managing their behavior. For some, behavior management plans and/or counseling services may be required. There are also classroom accommodations educators can make for students whether or not they have such behavior management plans and/or counseling services. For example, teachers can let students use study carrels or other enclosures to work independently with less distraction. Teachers can assign work that students are able to finish in shorter time durations. Teachers can also allow students to use timers to help them monitor how much more time they have to finish assignments and how much more time they need to complete their work. For students needing structure to promote behavioral self-control, teachers can positively reinforce following classroom rules, list consequences for breaking rules, and ensure students' knowledge of rules and consequences.

In addition to posting lists of classroom rules and consequences for breaking them and making sure all students know these, teachers can also make sure to supply students with activities to pursue during free time periods. Students requiring structure are apt to act out during unassigned times without the direction of something specific to do. To prepare students for transitions such as beginning new lessons, going to lunch, moving to other school areas, or changing classes, teachers should follow regular routines and give students prompts about the changes. Teachers may seat some students next to trained peers, teacher's aides, or volunteers to help them attend to lessons. They can also designate "study buddies" who know how to interact effectively with some students to help them when the teacher is otherwise occupied. For pupils who lack behavioral self-control without personal support and attention, the teacher can also conduct 1:1 instruction with certain students and work with others in small groups to address their needs.

Crisis Intervention and Prevention

In immediate responses to crises in schools, educators should concentrate on restoring equilibrium for students. Their demeanor should be calm, authoritative, and nurturing; their behaviors direct, informative, and oriented to problem-solving. Educators should address student denial by providing them with accurate information and realistic explanations about what happened and what they can expect. Reassurance should never be untrue or unrealistic. Educators should encourage students to face the factual aspects of a crisis. They should invite students to cope with their emotional responses, and discuss with them their responses and defense mechanisms. They should communicate to students a sense of positive expectations and hope, in that although crises bring changes, they have means of coping with these. Educators can shift students' positions from victims to actors by helping them plan appropriate, realistic, and salutary actions to follow after they separate, building upon demonstrated student coping skills and techniques, and when appropriate, engage them in helping restore equilibrium. They should link students with peers, family, and staff for immediate social support.

Three main elements of responding to and preventing crises in schools are: Communication; Direction and Coordination; and Health and Safety. During a crisis, educators communicate: they sound alarms if needed; clarify next steps; give information about the occurrence and first-aid

Copyright © Mometrix Media. You have been licensed one copy of this document for personal use only. Any other reproduction or redistribution is strictly prohibited. All rights reserved.
This content is provided for test preparation purposes only and does not imply an endorsement by Mometrix of any particular political, scientific, or religious point of view.

station locations, etc.; control rumors about the event; interact with the media as needed, and with the school district and community; respond to parent concerns; and keep track of the students and staff. Direction and coordination during a crisis include monitoring and solving problems and directing emergency operations centers. Health and safety during the emergency include directing evacuation, security, search and rescue operations; providing first aid for medical and psychological injuries; and reducing hazards to students and staff. Immediately after a crisis, communication includes dispelling rumors, clarifying crisis sources and impacts, and supplying information on medical and psychological resources available. Direction and coordination include continuing problem monitoring and solving. Health and safety include continuing activities begun during the crisis.

In the days and/or weeks following a school crisis, educators continue communication by supplying information and counseling to promote closure to students, school personnel, parents, and other school district and community members. They continue direction and coordination by monitoring and solving problems ensuing from the crisis. They continue health and safety by supplying case management, direct services, and/or referral for longer term treatments as needed to those involved. In efforts to prevent future crises, educators demonstrate communication by conducting debriefing meetings with school staff, parents, other community members, district personnel, and students as appropriate to make clear any deficits in their response to the recent crisis. They demonstrate direction and coordination by applying debriefing analysis to plan possible prevention of additional crises; limit the impacts of inevitable occurrences; and improve crisis response procedures and resources. They provide health and safety education to students, parents, and staff.

Difficulties in Reading and Following Instructional Methods

Many students with various disabilities have difficulties in the classroom due to problems they experience with following the instructional methods and reading and applying the textbooks and other printed or written learning materials used in regular education programs. Educators can help these students to work around such difficulties by providing them with accommodations. One of the most important skills to enable success in school is being able to read. However, many students who have disabilities are not reading at their grade level because of various impediments to their reading skills. Some are still in the process of acquiring fundamental skills in phonics (i.e., the relationship between speech sounds and the alphabetic letters that represent them) and word recognition. Some students are still in the process of learning how to apply techniques to assist them in comprehension of printed words, phrases, and sentences. In addition, plenty of textbooks, worksheets, and similar learning materials are not well-organized or clearly articulated, constituting further challenges to these students.

Accommodations for Students with Trouble Understanding Oral Presentations

Some students with disabilities have trouble deciphering what they are meant to learn from an oral lecture or discussion on an academic topic. Teachers can make such accommodations as visual aids, like supporting their oral presentations with overhead projectors, large charts, or blackboards. They can give students an overview of a lesson's content before presenting it, and also introduce students to new vocabulary words prior to the lesson. Immediately following an oral lesson or lecture, teachers can give a printed summary of its important points, accompanied by a list of questions for them to answer. To help students with difficulties following ideas in oral lectures and discussions, teachers can break up lectures with discussions or other activities in small groups, and also maintain student engagement by inviting their questions. They can identify the primary parts of steps in the information. They can write important ideas on chalkboards/whiteboards, emphasizing parts using different colors.

Copyright © Mometrix Media. You have been licensed one copy of this document for personal use only. Any other reproduction or redistribution is strictly prohibited. All rights reserved.
This content is provided for test preparation purposes only and does not imply an endorsement by Mometrix of any particular political, scientific, or religious point of view.

When students with various disabilities have trouble with taking notes on the teacher's oral lectures or lessons, the teacher can distribute printed copies of their lecture notes to accompany the oral presentation. They can allow these students to record orally presented class lessons, lectures, and discussions for their review and study. Teachers should repeat important concepts, paraphrase them to express them in more than one set of words, and provide students with summaries of all the most important points. It is especially helpful if teachers repeat, paraphrase, and summarize at the end of a lesson, lecture, or class discussion. Teachers can help students with taking notes by giving them copies of their overhead projector documents, diagrams, and/or outlines of their lectures. To reinforce the information in oral presentations, teachers should supplement them with charts, diagrams, written/printed text, and/or pictures, and repeat as frequently as needed. Also, for deaf or hard-of-hearing students, teachers should procure a sign-language interpreter or a note-taker.

Accommodations for Students with Trouble Learning Math

Some students who have various disabilities have deficient skills in basic arithmetic and may still depend on counting on their fingers beyond the usual age. Some students with disabilities have major problems with remembering fundamental facts related to math. For students who have trouble with understanding mathematical concepts and solving math problems, teachers can provide accommodations such as giving them concrete objects and materials to assist in learning math concepts. Many students who cannot understand abstract ideas solely through mental processes can succeed better when they can process them using concrete, tangible things they can see, touch, and manipulate. Teachers can also highlight or color-code the important words in mathematical word problems for students. They can allow students to utilize charts to plan how they will solve math problems. And they can permit students to use basic fact charts and/or calculators to follow formulas and compute numbers for solving math problems.

Accommodations for Students with Trouble Reading

One common problem for students with disabilities is isolating the main ideas in a book they are reading and/or which parts are important to remember. Teachers can highlight the important concepts and instruct students to read these first. They can give study guides to students for independent reading. They can offer students books on the same subjects at lower grade levels to make the main ideas easier to identify. Some students comprehend information when they hear it, but cannot read it. Teachers can supply books on tape/recorded versions; videos or movies of the information; computer text-to-speech software programs; and/or assign classmates to read printed materials aloud to students. Students with blindness or visual impairments may need specially produced materials and/or equipment to access class information. Teachers can supply books on tape or texts with large print; books and other materials in Braille or embossed formats; and give students equipment like magnifying devices or optical enhancers.

Accommodations for Students Who Have Trouble with Handwriting

Students with a number of different disabilities can have difficulty with the fine motor control involved in handwriting. In general, the same kinds of classroom accommodations are required to address disabled student needs for both written assignments and written tests. For example, if a student needs to complete a written assignment using a word processor, s/he will also need the word processor to complete a written test. For students having difficulties with fine motor control, teachers can allow them to write straight into their workbooks instead of on separate paper or on photocopies of the workbook pages. They can permit students to type on typewriters, word processors, or computer keyboards. They can arrange for students to dictate their assignment and/or test responses to scribes, like classmates or teaching assistants, who write down their dictations. Teachers can also allow and provide adaptive equipment for students, such as special

Copyright © Mometrix Media. You have been licensed one copy of this document for personal use only. Any other reproduction or redistribution is strictly prohibited. All rights reserved.
This content is provided for test preparation purposes only and does not imply an endorsement by Mometrix of any particular political, scientific, or religious point of view.

pen/pencil holders or grips, pens with erasable ink, and special paper featuring raised/embossed lines or color-coded line ruling.

Accommodations for Students Who Have Trouble with Expressive Language

Many students with disabilities may have good ideas, but have difficulties with expressing these in writing and/or speech. Teachers can provide them with accommodations that can facilitate their use of expressive language. For example, they can allow students to use a thesaurus to look up words that express the ideas they want to convey, and to find additional synonyms and antonyms for words if their actual vocabularies and/or their access to retrieving words they know are limited. Teachers can allow and provide to students specialized word-processing software programs that predict the words that students are trying to express. They can allow students to make use of electronic spelling aids and/or spelling dictionaries to support correct orthography. Teachers should also grade the content of written assignments separately from the writing mechanics in academic subjects (other than English composition, grammar, or spelling). They should additionally allow students with disabilities to correct their grammatical and spelling errors when they are completing written assignments or assessments.

Accommodations for Students Who Have Trouble Completing Assigned Work

Some students with disabilities can do the same work as others, but much more slowly. This can cause them to run out of time to finish assignments. Other students have trouble remembering to assemble the materials and resources they will need to complete assignments. For students who have trouble keeping track of their class assignments, teachers can provide accommodations by dividing longer assignments into portions and giving students separate due dates for each portion. Teachers can instruct students to mark their assignments' due dates on a calendar they can see. To accommodate students who work more slowly than others, teachers can assign a smaller total amount of work, while still ensuring that the items or tasks they choose are those necessary for meeting all the learning objectives they have identified. Teachers can allow these students to use instructional materials and resources outside of class. Until students can complete assignments on time, teachers can provide them with reinforcement via partial credit for incomplete or late work.

Accommodations on Tests

Five main categories wherein accommodations are permitted on standardized tests are presentation, response, schedule, setting, and assistive technology. Insofar as they are legally allowed on standardized tests, students with disabilities generally need the same kinds of accommodations for classroom and standardized assessments. Accommodations enable students to demonstrate their mastery of skills and knowledge without their disabilities interfering. For students with reading deficits, teachers can read test items aloud to them (excluding reading skills tests). They can supply text-to-speech software to present students with test directions and/or nonreading test items. They can let students read test items to themselves instead of presenting them orally. They can supply Braille or large-print test forms, and/or visual magnifiers, auditory amplifiers, or other assistive technology. To aid in focusing visually on tests, teachers can have students use positioning tools, pointers, blank cards, templates, colored, blank overlays, or transparencies. To decrease auditory distraction, they can give students headphones and "white noise" machines.

Accommodating Students Who Have Trouble Following Directions

In general, teachers speak, write, or demonstrate to students what they want them to do in school. Some students with disabilities have difficulty attending to spoken, written, or demonstrated information; some with remembering it; and some with both attending and retaining it. Moreover, some students with disabilities have difficulty comprehending and/or applying directions. When

Copyright © Mometrix Media. You have been licensed one copy of this document for personal use only. Any other reproduction or redistribution is strictly prohibited. All rights reserved.
This content is provided for test preparation purposes only and does not imply an endorsement by Mometrix of any particular political, scientific, or religious point of view.

students find it hard to remember what they were instructed to do, teachers can provide accommodations by asking them to repeat the instructions in their own words or to demonstrate physically what they were instructed to do. They can also teach these students how to use personal planners or assignment notebooks for keeping track of assignments and tests. When students have difficulty comprehending the teacher's instructions, the teacher can provide accommodations by giving directions broken down into consecutive steps, and furnishing pictures or outlines of them. They can demonstrate for students how to complete sample tasks or problems, and combine oral instructions with pictures, diagrams, and/or printed words.

When students with disabilities are taking classroom and/or standardized tests, they can often have difficulty with accessing, understanding, and/or following the directions in the tests. Teachers can provide classroom accommodations to these students to facilitate test-taking. For example, they can provide answer forms or test forms with visual symbols, like stop signs, arrows, etc., to guide students in following directions. Some standardized tests already include such symbols for all students. When test directions are presented orally, teachers can provide sign language interpreters for deaf or hard-of-hearing students. When test directions and writing prompts are presented in print, teachers can read these aloud for students with visual impairments, cognitive disabilities, and reading-related learning disabilities. For students who need it, teachers can reread test directions or further explain their meaning. Teachers can also highlight or underline the most important words in test directions and/or test items for students with disabilities.

Accommodating Students Who Have Problems with Organization

Students with attention deficits, cognitive impairments, and other disabilities can be distracted more easily than usual, causing them to confuse or forget the teacher's instructions. Students who find it hard to pay attention to more than one thing at a time frequently encounter difficulty completing complex assignments. Compounding these, some instructional materials are unclear by nature, and materials with excessive details can cause disabled students great confusion. Additionally, many disabled students have trouble storing, finding, and keeping track of classroom materials. Teachers can provide accommodations for confusion with complexity in materials and instructions by color-coding different materials or tasks to help students identify them. They should arrange tasks in clear, uncluttered formats with obvious beginning points and step sequences. To help students keep their materials organized, teachers can provide them with special binders or folders with dividers and different colors for each subject and unit. Teachers can also provide students with checklists of the materials they need for each class, which students keep in/on their binders, desks, or lockers.

Accommodations for Students Who Have Difficulty Understanding Test Directions

When students with disabilities are not sure what to do on tests, teachers should avoid hinting at right/wrong answers but still accommodate them verbally by encouraging them (e.g., to answer each question and continue working), and they should give them additional examples of test items for practice to ensure they know what to do during actual testing. Most standardized tests prohibit accommodations in presentation that alter the assessed skill; for example, if a test measures reading skills, teachers cannot read items aloud to students. However, certain accommodations are permissible for classroom assessments. For students having difficulty switching among task types, teachers can group similar items and place easiest items first on tests. They can divide matching tasks into smaller groups of 4 to 5 items each. For essay/fill-in-the-blank items, they can provide applicable word lists. Whenever memorization is not required, teachers can let students take open-book tests. On multiple-choice tests, teachers can remove one choice from each question. Teachers can select test questions covering all content required but give fewer total questions.

Copyright © Mometrix Media. You have been licensed one copy of this document for personal use only. Any other reproduction or redistribution is strictly prohibited. All rights reserved.
This content is provided for test preparation purposes only and does not imply an endorsement by Mometrix of any particular political, scientific, or religious point of view.

Accommodations for Students Who Have Trouble Sustaining Attention on Tests

When administering state standardized tests, teachers may provide some accommodations to disabled students who struggle to maintain their attention and energy during testing. For example, teachers may monitor student answer sheets to see whether they are putting their responses in the right places. When student responses to extended-response items are partly correct, teachers may give partial credit as designated by the rubrics for these items on state standardized achievement tests. In classroom assessments, teachers may furnish students with prepared outlines, charts, diagrams, and/or webs to help them plan essay or open-ended question responses. Students may demonstrate their skills and knowledge via alternate formats like role-plays, oral interviews, or physical demonstrations. They may be allowed references like thesauruses, dictionaries, or almanacs. They may be allowed concrete manipulatives to do and/or check calculations. Students may retake tests and get credit for improving. Also, some state standardized tests even allow certain grades to retake them.

Accommodations Students May Need Regarding Location of Test

Some students with special needs are so easily distracted that they cannot perform to their ability if they take a test in a large group. Accommodations to address this problem include administering the test to the student in isolation or in a smaller group; allowing the student to take the test in a study carrel or other enclosure; or having the student take the test in another room free of distractions. Other students have physical or sensory disabilities that have an impact on their ability to take a test. In such cases, schools and teachers need to allow these students to use whatever adaptive equipment or furniture they require to be able to participate in the assessment. One important consideration in allowing the use of assistive technology is that it does not alter the performance of the actual skills being tested. For example, if a test measures skills in reading printed language, a student could not use text-to-speech software for that particular test.

Accommodations Students May Need for Providing Test Answers

Students with various disabilities can have difficulty handwriting test answers, circling or checking multiple-choice answers, filling in bubbles, or solving problems and explaining their solutions. Accommodations often allowed on standardized tests in some states include giving additional space for students to handwrite their answers; allowing students to answer questions orally instead of in writing, to dictate their answers into a sound recorder, or to a scribe or test proctor; or allowing the student to sign his or her test responses to a sign-language interpreter. Students may also be permitted to use word processors or computer or typewriter keyboards to answer test questions, although state standardized tests typically prohibit their using spell-check and grammar-check software when typing. Students may write into their test booklets instead of on separate sheets, create Braille answers on separate paper, or record their answers using speech-to-text software programs. Students are also often allowed to use outlines, charts, and/or diagrams for planning essay or open-ended question responses on tests.

Assistive Technology

Students with various disabilities may need assistive technology to acquire the information they are expected to learn and/or to communicate what they have learned. As long as the purpose of assessment is not defeated, the skills being assessed are not changed, and the student's responses still reflect his or her independent efforts, students can generally use the same assistive technology they use during classroom instruction to complete assessments. For example, a student with a disability might be given an accommodation allowing him or her to use an adaptive calculator for solving mathematics problems on a test. Some state standardized achievement tests allow students in seventh through tenth grades, for example, to use calculators. Another example involves

Copyright © Mometrix Media. You have been licensed one copy of this document for personal use only. Any other reproduction or redistribution is strictly prohibited. All rights reserved.
This content is provided for test preparation purposes only and does not imply an endorsement by Mometrix of any particular political, scientific, or religious point of view.

completing answers to essay questions and/or long explanations or answers to questions on tests. Students with disabilities may be permitted to use assistive technology, such as voice recorders to dictate their responses, or word processors to type them.

Accommodations Regarding Test Schedule

Some students with disabilities need additional time to finish taking a test. Students who work very slowly, those who can work for only briefer periods at a time, and those using certain types of assistive technology may need alterations in testing schedules. Accommodations when administering typical state standardized tests include allowing longer times for students to take the test; dividing a test into smaller portions and allowing students to take each portion on a different day if necessary; permitting students to take short breaks during the testing period; and allowing students to take a test at different times of day if physical conditions and/or medications affect their alertness and attention. Teachers may provide additional accommodations not allowed on standardized tests for classroom assessments. For example, the teacher can give disabled students fewer test questions, as long as they still cover all the same skills and content being assessed. Teachers may also let students review and correct their test answers from the day before.

Unusual or Unique Test Accommodations Required by Some Students

Some students can have disabilities that necessitate more unusual accommodations in order to participate in state standardized achievement testing. Testing accommodations identified as unique usually entail some changes in the existing assessment materials. Typically, states will allow such unique assessment accommodations if their Commissioner of Education has previously approved their use. Parents and teachers can look to the program of educational services to exceptional students in their school district to assist them with making a request for approval of such accommodations. Several examples of unique or unusual accommodations that may be approved for students with disabilities to participate in standardized assessments include: test forms with fewer items on each page; test forms with more space separating each item from the next; test forms with modified or tabbed pages to enable students to turn pages more easily; and having test question and response forms attached to the student's work area to prevent their falling, sliding, or shifting to facilitate reading and writing or marking on them.

Adapting Class Schedules and Time Constraints

Many students with disabilities learn and/or work at slower speeds than their nondisabled peers. Others perform better without the pressure of rigorous schedules. Teachers can provide them with time- and schedule-related accommodations. For example, some high school students may be given an Incomplete course grade and finish the course in summer school or the next semester. On practice assignments with multiple similar items, students who have the cognitive ability to learn without excessive repetition but need additional time and/or perform poorly under time pressure may be permitted to complete only every other item. Another educator consideration regarding students with disabilities is that in middle school and high school programs, it is particularly critical to assign these students to classes appropriate for them. Teachers of special education are advised that they may facilitate this process by working with their school administrators to ensure that the schedules of assigned classes are able to accommodate the special needs of any students who have disabilities.

Some students who have disabilities can handle the same course content as their peers, but they need more time to do so, or they need their work to be broken up into shorter time periods with breaks in between. Some students with disabilities suffer deterioration in their performance when they feel pressured by time limits. Some also require more time to complete assignments and assessments due to the adaptive equipment they must use in order to participate. Some strategies

Copyright © Mometrix Media. You have been licensed one copy of this document for personal use only. Any other reproduction or redistribution is strictly prohibited. All rights reserved.
This content is provided for test preparation purposes only and does not imply an endorsement by Mometrix of any particular political, scientific, or religious point of view.

teachers can use include keeping schedules flexible to allow students with disabilities more time to finish a course. This can include completing the requirements in summer school. Teachers can allow students with disabilities extra time to complete their classwork and take tests. They can assign work further in advance to allow students with disabilities a chance to begin their assignments earlier. Teachers can also supply students with clear schedules of all units, assignments, and tests, and include periodic checkpoints within these schedules to help students monitor their progress.

NIMAS

The IDEA incorporates the National Instructional Materials Accessibility Standard or NIMAS. The stated purpose of this standard is to "facilitate the provision of accessible, alternate-format versions of print textbooks to pre-K–12 students with disabilities." This standard provides information to assist school IEP teams in deciding how they can electronically provide access to textbooks and other reading materials to students who have dyslexia and other LDs with reading. Parents who have children with reading disabilities should look at their children's IEPs and/or 504 plans to discover whether they contain anything about eligibility for accessible instructional materials, or AIM. If a student was determined not to be eligible for AIM, parents have the legal right to talk with their school personnel about why not. Parents can advocate for their children with schools by initiating conversations about how their children learn best, and how alternative formats, digital software, and/or readers can sometimes strikingly improve their learning and their motivation and confidence in it.

AIM

AIM stands for Accessible Instructional Materials. Many students with disabilities find reading impossible or difficult because of various disabilities affecting being able to read standard printed materials. AIMs consist of textbooks and other printed educational materials published in special digital formats. These formats provide accommodation to individuals who are blind, visually impaired, have various physical disabilities, and have reading-related learning disabilities (LDs) including dyslexia. Using digital formats enables students with reading and/or print disabilities to hear and see the text simultaneously using a computer, tablet, or other digital device. AIM includes formats like Braille, large print, audio, and digital text. The standard format for digital text files is named DAISY, for Digital Accessible Information System. DAISY allows users to listen to recordings of human voices or electronic speech synthesizers for audio versions of print materials. Accompanying reading software presents text visually at the same time. Today, most young students are comfortable and familiar with electronic voices and adapt easily to using them for reading.

Resources Providing Accessible Text Formats

Two organizations whose specialty is providing accessible text formats are Bookshare at bookshare.org and Learning Ally at learningally.org. Bookshare is an online library of over 150,000 digital versions of copyrighted textbooks and other books. Learning Ally is an online library of more than 70,000 audio versions of literary works and textbooks, with both recordings of human voices and digitally synthesized voices reading the material. These organizations both have approval from the US Department of Education for providing accessible instructional materials (AIM) to school districts and individual schools. Schools and/or districts can request digital formats or files from these groups for qualifying students with reading or print disabilities. Due to their cooperative missions, qualified members of either organization can more easily gain membership in the other. Some school districts or schools even pay for memberships in both organizations or either one for students who are found eligible.

Copyright © Mometrix Media. You have been licensed one copy of this document for personal use only. Any other reproduction or redistribution is strictly prohibited. All rights reserved.
This content is provided for test preparation purposes only and does not imply an endorsement by Mometrix of any particular political, scientific, or religious point of view.

Research Evidence Regarding Text-to-Speech Technology

Studies suggest that reading technologies that use audio or digital formats can enhance the reading process for students with learning disabilities. When students simultaneously see words and sentences highlighted on the screens of computers, tablets, or other devices and hear them read aloud via text-to-speech (TTS) programs, this is described as "multisensory" or "multimodal" reading. With digital education widespread today, students may learn at home or while on the go as well as in the classroom. In this environment, AT programs are compatible with student learning processes. Some high-quality programs include Read Write Gold by TextHelp; Read: OutLoud by Don Johnston; and Kurzweil 3000 by Cambium. For iPads and other Apple devices, the large online digital library Bookshare offers an application ("app") called Read2Go, which enables its members to download and read its digital books on their devices. Students can digitally navigate through books' tables of contents, chapters, pages, and paragraphs.

Challenges in Converting Elements in Print Books to Digital Formats

According to the National Center for Learning Disabilities, certain visual images in printed books—for example, mathematical concepts, charts, and graphs—cannot be accurately represented using text-to-speech software programs. This presents a limitation to what students with reading or other disabilities can access compared to the original printed book versions. However, progress in technology is addressing this need. The organization Benetech is the parent group of the extensive online library known as Bookshare (bookshare.org). Benetech has a division called the DIAGRAM Center. At the DIAGRAM Center, designers of digital technology have created a new web application tool named POET. POET is an open-source application that enables crowd sourcing of verbal descriptions of visual images. In addition, it facilitates the process of creating descriptions of visual images for Digital Accessible Information System or DAISY file format, the standard format for digital text files. The progress of this and similar technology developments afford increased access to text for students with disabilities.

Research Findings Concerning Instruction of Literacy, Math, and Science

Comprehensive literature reviews find nearly twice as much research exists about teaching literacy as math, and four times more about math than science. One commonality among these areas is that using behavior analysis principles is effective for teaching them all to severely developmentally disabled students. For example, using task analysis to break down the instruction of multistep (chained) tasks and using time delay for teaching separate tasks are both highly effective for teaching academic content. These techniques are used in systematic instruction, which studies show is an effective overall teaching strategy for these students. Systematic instruction has been used to teach feeding, toileting, dressing, safety, and many other functional skills, and academic skills as well. Systematic instruction procedures define observable, measurable target skills; collect intervention data to prove new skill acquisition; apply behavioral principles and techniques like systematic prompts and fading, error correction, and differential reinforcement to aid transfer of learned skills; and effect behavioral changes that can be generalized across skills, materials, people, and contexts.

Digital Books

Today, students can download and read books digitally on tablets, other devices, and computers from online digital libraries, which even offer apps (applications) for downloading to digital devices. Students can interact with, manipulate, and change settings in digital reading matter, including the sizes and colors of the fonts, both in the text and in hypertext links; choosing between male or female voices in audio versions of text; adjusting the speed of the readers' speech in audio text; turning on and off the read-aloud function in books with both visual and audio text; setting

Copyright © Mometrix Media. You have been licensed one copy of this document for personal use only. Any other reproduction or redistribution is strictly prohibited. All rights reserved.
This content is provided for test preparation purposes only and does not imply an endorsement by Mometrix of any particular political, scientific, or religious point of view.

bookmarks in books; and changing the appearances of background displays in digital books. Some software programs and portable devices incorporate graphic organizers to aid comprehension and studying; note-taking tools to aid in essay writing; built-in scanners to copy and upload/download documents and pictures; support tools for outline writing; dictionaries, spell-checkers; keyword searches; bibliographers; voice recorders, voice recognition; and Acapela Voices, which reads text aloud translated into Spanish and other languages for ESL/ELL students.

Effective Instruction in Reading

According to the National Reading Panel, three main components of effective instruction in reading are (1) phonemic awareness, phonics, and alphabet knowledge; (2) vocabulary, text comprehension, and reading fluency; and (3) reading comprehension strategies. When the National Center for Learning Disabilities surveyed teachers and assistive technology (AT) specialists about digital technologies and digital books, the consensus of their responses identified a number of benefits. These included that digital reading technology affords a whole new world of learning potential for students, and that it affords flexibility among more learning options according to student preferences and learning styles. Teachers and AT specialists also find that digital reading options further the personal achievement, independence, and socialization skills of students. They say digital reading does much to aid students who struggle with decoding printed words. It keeps students' attention for longer time spans. It helps students read at their grade levels. It encourages students to take notes and make annotations to texts. And it corrects students' spelling errors.

Evidence-Based Strategies for Teaching Science

Recent educational research studies have shown that teachers, when trained in a specific task analysis, could teach developmentally disabled students to conduct science experiments. Some researchers have used graphic organizers to teach science core content to students with autism in middle school. Others taught science vocabulary and concepts to similar students using explicit instruction of descriptors. And some have taught the steps of scientific inquiry lessons, and science concepts that the learners generalized to new materials, to students with moderate intellectual disabilities. Research has shown that time delay and similar strategies for special educators to teach math and science vocabulary across multiple academic content areas is effective with high school students having moderate and severe developmental disabilities. Other researchers have recently investigated teaching early science concepts and vocabulary to elementary school students with severe DDs. They find even at lower ages/grades and more severe disabilities, students learned comprehension of both scientific vocabulary and concepts, meeting the criteria of state standards for progress through science lessons in the general education curriculum.

ESL Classes

American classrooms where students are learning English as a new language demand much more interaction between students and teachers than other classrooms generally do. Many activities assigned in ESL classes involve group work, which necessitates moving desks, getting up, and moving around, which must be kept in mind for disabled students. Teachers should also be sensitive to the diversity of most ESL classes, which often include students from different countries and of various ages. ESL teachers can help by educating themselves in advance about any specific disabilities incoming students to their classes have. They should ensure their classes are inclusive, by providing accommodations and/or services needed by disabled students, and communicating this to students clearly in their course syllabi and in other ways. They should discuss with disabled students how their needs and accommodations might change, and any help or adjustments such changes could necessitate.

Copyright © Mometrix Media. You have been licensed one copy of this document for personal use only. Any other reproduction or redistribution is strictly prohibited. All rights reserved.
This content is provided for test preparation purposes only and does not imply an endorsement by Mometrix of any particular political, scientific, or religious point of view.

Approach to Having Disabled Students in ESL Classroom

ESL teachers with disabled students should discuss their needs and accommodations with the students. They should also discuss these with their teaching assistants, aides, school office staff, and other support staff, and also request that they help with accommodations for these students. Teachers must observe privacy regulations and not disclose disability information with faculty, staff, or other students, except in regard to accommodations that are needed. In the United States, the law requires schools, agencies, and other organizations to provide the same accommodations to international students with disabilities as they do to US citizens; ESL teachers in America should comply with this legal requirement. All world nations have organizations that provide access to local resources for people with disabilities. ESL teachers with disabled students can contact these groups for resources and advice. Regardless of the type of disability, teachers should concentrate on the individual student's abilities and strengths.

Depending on the type and extent of a disability and the classroom situation, students with various disabilities can find everyday classroom activities difficult, e.g., active learning that involves getting up and engaging in different physical actions; making physical and oral presentations; or participating in group or class discussions. ESL teachers can exercise their creativity by adapting the activities they design and assign to allow more universal student access, while still attaining the same learning goals. When an ESL teacher has a student with a disability in the class, the teacher should communicate the same expectations and standards for academic achievement and personal behavior that s/he has for all students. The majority of students with disabilities appreciate being treated with the same educational standards and teacher expectations as a sign of respect from the teacher. ESL teachers should also ask their disabled students regularly for feedback about what things in class work and do not work for them, and how things that do not work may be adjusted or modified.

Communication Skills and Instruction for Blind or Visually Impaired Students

While teachers routinely use visual aids like pictures, flash cards, graphs, charts, and pointing at objects in the room while saying "this" or "that," they must realize these are not accessible to blind or visually impaired students. They must provide them with additional tactile versions and/or verbal descriptions. Students with low vision may not be able to see writing on blackboards/whiteboards, in workbooks, etc. They should be seated at the front of the room and allowed to bring their own magnifying devices. Before class, teachers can provide handouts to these students in Braille, large print, audio formats, or electronic formats depending on their preferred format, and/or give students additional prompts during class. When presenting visual information, teachers should spell new vocabulary words aloud; print using large, clear letters; use larger sized fonts in overheads and handouts; and read aloud as they write, which benefits all students. When drawing or displaying pictures, teachers should verbally describe their contents.

Equal Access to Classroom Content for Students with Low Vision or Blindness

When school assignments involve large amounts of reading, students with low vision often experience eye fatigue and need to rest their eyes frequently. Teachers can permit them breaks during class and/or give them extensions on due dates for reading assignments. Teachers should ensure student access to alternative media formats like Braille, audio recordings, or large print. Some students bring laptops or other computerized devices with text-to-speech, large print, or Braille conversion software; teachers should provide their teaching content in electronic formats for these students. They should also discuss with them whether any websites the teacher uses as lesson supplements are incompatible with students' special software, and consider adjusting their curriculum to use compatible sites. Teachers should also keep classroom layout consistent to facilitate student orientation and navigation. Teachers sharing classrooms can try to enlist the other

Copyright © Mometrix Media. You have been licensed one copy of this document for personal use only. Any other reproduction or redistribution is strictly prohibited. All rights reserved.
This content is provided for test preparation purposes only and does not imply an endorsement by Mometrix of any particular political, scientific, or religious point of view.

teachers' cooperation and assistance. Tactile and/or audio rather than visual cues more effectively get these students' attention. Teachers can also instruct other students to say their names before speaking during group discussions.

Considerations for Students with Mobility Disabilities

When assigning group activities, teachers may need more flexibility and time for assembling groups and moving furniture. Teachers should consider this in assigning groups/pairs, without restricting variety among student partners/classmates. Students with limited/no use of their arms cannot perform common classroom behaviors like jotting down new vocabulary words, looking words up in dictionaries or encyclopedias, or even raising their hands. Teachers need to provide them with alternative methods, like a scribe to take notes, orally saying "yes"/"no" instead of raising hands, etc. Teachers can collaborate with students on alternative means to get teacher attention. Students in wheelchairs may arrive late and/or need to leave early because of weather, transportation service, architectural barriers, or other factors outside their control. Teachers should discuss with students whether their disability requiring accommodation or behavioral factors cause late arrivals/early departures, defining expectations and resolving issues accordingly. Teachers should ensure other students realize wheelchairs/other adaptive equipment constitute personal space and respect it. Teachers and students should sit when interacting with students of shorter stature or students in wheelchairs.

Instructional Considerations for Deaf and Hard-of-Hearing Students

Some deaf/hard-of-hearing students learn written English and speech reading to understand hearing people, but communicate using sign language and do not learn speech. Others want to learn speech and have pronunciation difficulties due to their hearing loss. For students who want to use spoken English, teachers can find technological help. For example, microphones equipped with FM systems not only amplify speech sounds, but also send them directly to the student's hearing aids. Teachers can also repeat what other students say if they are out of microphone range, which benefits all students. For deaf students who communicate using sign language, teachers can engage the services of sign language interpreters; they can additionally learn several simpler signs themselves to facilitate basic communication with these students. Interpreting can be challenging for international students, because sign language is not universal but varies among countries. In this case, speech-to-text services may be better. Teachers should always directly address the student rather than the sign language interpreter/STT assistant.

Even deaf/HOH students who use spoken English are apt to have problems during class activities involving faster reaction times, like listen-and-repeat exercises. Teachers can give them more time to repeat, and also try to eliminate background noises—including cross-talk from other students—as possible. Fire alarms, other audio emergency signals, and PA speaker announcements are not usually accessible to deaf students. Teachers can accommodate them by flicking the overhead lights on and off, waving a hand, or touching them on the shoulder to get their attention before announcements or during alarms. Viewing videos of movies and TV programs is an activity often used and enjoyed in classrooms in general and even more so in ESL classes. However, teachers should be sure the videos include English closed captions or subtitles. This benefits comprehension for both deaf/HOH and ESL students. If captions/subtitles are unavailable for a video, teachers can procure sign language interpreters or speech-to-text note-takers. HOH students often comprehend video images better than audio practice.

Teachers should seek means of utilizing visual aids as supplements to all their lessons. They should wait to allow time for students to view both the signs of a sign language interpreter or the text of speech-to-text software programs, and also the visual aid the teacher presents. Teachers should be

Copyright © Mometrix Media. You have been licensed one copy of this document for personal use only. Any other reproduction or redistribution is strictly prohibited. All rights reserved.
This content is provided for test preparation purposes only and does not imply an endorsement by Mometrix of any particular political, scientific, or religious point of view.

mindful whether they are standing between the student and interpreter. Teachers can also use color-coding, e.g., different pen colors to represent different parts of a sentence—like red for subjects or blue for verbs. They can use geometric shapes to adapt concepts visually and use their fingers to represent different subjects or different tenses when conjugating verbs. Since some deaf/hard-of-hearing students speech read, teachers should not stand in front of windows or other places that interfere with this. Seating in front of the room or circular seating wherein students can see both the teacher and classmates can help hearing-impaired students always see who is speaking. Decreasing background noise from open windows, large groups, fans, or cross-talk helps students follow class discussions.

Considerations for Students with Chronic Health and Mental Health Disabilities

Some students have different conditions like diabetes, asthma, seizure disorder, multiple sclerosis, arthritis, or anxiety, depression, obsessive-compulsive disorder, or bipolar disorder. Individual differences in symptoms complicate such chronic disabilities. Due to the condition, medication side effects, and/or the environment, students may feel/perform better/worse at certain times of the day/on certain days. This can influence attendance, attention, and memory. Teachers should permit students flexibility in taking breaks, extend time for finishing assignments, allow note-takers, adjust schedules, and let students make up missed tests as necessary. Some students with chronic conditions need rest at home for days/weeks, but may be able to study and do homework there. Teachers can design and adhere to a good syllabus to inform students what to do if they miss classes. Some students have sensitivities to sensory stimuli like temperature changes, lights, or sounds, or they have other conditions affecting classroom participation and/or social interactions. Teachers should make time to acquaint themselves with each student's unique circumstances and which accommodations help them most.

Teaching Communication Skills to Students with Speech Disabilities

Some students have difficulty controlling their speech muscles secondary to cerebral palsy; some progressive illnesses cause speech problems; and traumatic brain injuries can cause aphasia, a language processing problem. Some students stutter, and some have voice disorders secondary to cleft palate/lip, vocal nodules/polyps, etc. Students who cannot speak functionally use electronic voice synthesizers or visual-manual communication boards/books. Others can speak, but less quickly, clearly and/or fluently than normal. Many students have milder articulation disorders that still affect their communication. Teachers not understanding a student should not say/pretend they do, but allow them to repeat; they are accustomed to it. Teachers should not finish their sentences for them, but give them time for self-expression, promoting self-confidence. Teachers must adjust their expectations for oral assignments/tests. They can also seek alternative means for students to attain class goals, e.g., hand-raising, writing, or group-texting question answers and slower discussion speeds. For students with communications assistants, teachers should address the student, not the assistant.

Teaching Strategies for Students with Cognitive and Learning Disabilities

Students with learning and cognitive disabilities are increasingly common in today's classrooms and quite common in ESL classrooms where they can substantially affect how students learn English. Standard instructional methods for language are usually less effective for students with learning disabilities, autism spectrum disorders (ASDs), and various other neurological deficits. Teachers are responsible for modifying their teaching styles to facilitate learning, and ESL teachers to facilitate learning a new language. In ESL, students with LDs must not only process words and symbols; they also contend with various difficulties remembering/retrieving words, articulating speech sounds, fluency, organizing thoughts, constructing sentences, and thinking abstractly. Teachers should focus not on student deficits, but strategies many students have developed

Copyright © Mometrix Media. You have been licensed one copy of this document for personal use only. Any other reproduction or redistribution is strictly prohibited. All rights reserved.
This content is provided for test preparation purposes only and does not imply an endorsement by Mometrix of any particular political, scientific, or religious point of view.

independently to compensate. Teachers can provide accommodations like more time for activities and tests; note-takers; and tutors. Neurological deficits that affect social skills, as with ASDs, can make group/pair activities challenging. Teachers should provide structure and lead classes deliberately, clarifying the goals and purposes of each segment of the class.

An ESL teacher may find that students with traumatic brain injuries or ADHD encounter difficulty in class, especially if the teacher presents information using only one format, modality, or approach. Teachers should use multimodal teaching approaches and alternative assessment formats. Utilizing a variety of instructional methods, e.g., lectures, games, small group assignments, or paired work, will make it easier for these students to find which technique(s) are most effective for them. Students with LDs often perform better in one modality and worse in another, e.g., excelling at spoken skills but struggling with written skills. Teachers can accommodate these students by offering them a variety of ways to demonstrate their learning, like doing assignments in artistic or oral formats. Teachers should also realize that individual differences give every student's neurological deficit a unique presentation, so they must discover solutions case by case. ESL teachers need to understand students' abilities/skills in their native languages to differentiate errors due to disabilities from those naturally due to learning a second language.

Self-Confidence in Disabled Students

Many students with disabilities are aware of their disability, which can undermine their self-confidence. They often feel they are different and do not fit in socially and have experienced rejection, ridicule, and bullying by other students. Additionally, experiencing failure at tasks their nondisabled peers complete easily can lower their self-esteem. Teachers can offer explicit instruction, asking students to identify good qualities they possess; help them develop positive affirmations they can understand, repeat, and believe; and provide plentiful positive reinforcement for every small success and for admirable efforts regardless of outcome. They can have students describe how they think others see them, and collaborate to develop strategies to improve their own and others' images of them. They can teach students to accept and offer praise and criticism appropriately with others. Students may also need training in wearing clothing appropriate to different social situations and answering and using telephones properly. The more students master such social skills, the more self-confidence they will develop.

Personal and Social Skills

For all people with and without disabilities, it can be challenging to get along with others. One of the commonest reasons that adults are fired from jobs and students have problems in school is inadequate social and personal skills. Students with various disabilities that affect learning often do not learn through observation and imitation as others do. Teachers need to instruct them explicitly in areas like self-awareness. They must teach them to identify their own physical and psychological needs, abilities, interests, and emotions by asking them questions; showing them how to point to pictures representing various feelings, actions, events; or teaching them descriptive vocabulary. Teachers need to guide students to learn to identify and demonstrate knowledge of their physical beings and their relationship to and interaction with space, objects, and other people. They need to help students properly utilize, care for, and maintain hearing aids, glasses, braces, crutches, wheelchairs, or walkers. Teachers can also help disabled students learn appropriate strategies for coping with life stressors.

For students with disabilities to interact well with their classmates and others, one key area is in social conversations as well as in class discussions. Students must learn both to listen to others, which includes not only refraining from interrupting them, but also listening attentively to what they say, and to respond appropriately to what others say. Students with intellectual disabilities

Copyright © Mometrix Media. You have been licensed one copy of this document for personal use only. Any other reproduction or redistribution is strictly prohibited. All rights reserved.
This content is provided for test preparation purposes only and does not imply an endorsement by Mometrix of any particular political, scientific, or religious point of view.

may, for example, change the subject completely instead of saying something that continues the topic. Teachers can give explicit instruction. For example, they can ask the student to repeat or paraphrase what another student just said; then ask her/him what possible things s/he could say in return on the same topic; have her/him demonstrate; and give positive reinforcement. Another area is forming and maintaining close relationships and friendships with others. Teachers can counsel students by asking them who shares particular interests, activities, and/or personal characteristics with them; helping them identify and implement behaviors for establishing and keeping relationships and friendships; and monitoring their progress by inquiring periodically.

Some students with cognitive disabilities may not have a good sense of personal possessions and boundaries. Consequently, they may take others' belongings; not take turns with others; or go ahead of others in lines. One facet of socially responsible behavior is respecting others' property and rights. Teachers can point out other students' showing such respect; explicitly show intellectually disabled students how to do the same; and give ample positive reinforcement whenever they do. Students with behavior disorders like oppositional defiant disorder will defy/ignore authority and directions. Teachers can establish behavioral contracts with them whereby they gain rewards meaningful to them for complying with clearly defined terms of what to do and not do. Students with ADHD easily act on impulse and become distracted, interfering with following directions. Behavior modification techniques or cognitive-behavioral therapy, sometimes in conjunction with medication, can help. Students also must learn to recognize valuable personal characteristics (e.g., honesty, kindness, or bravery); their personal roles in society; and social etiquette and proper behavior in public.

Independence for Students with Disabilities

Many students with disabilities have had things done for them that they could not accomplish alone and may have become habituated to passively waiting for others to initiate activities. Educators can help them achieve more independence by first explicitly teaching a student needed skills, giving prompts for each step, and then systematically fading the prompts so the student gradually performs tasks/activities with less and less help, direction, and guidance. Depending on the disability and activity, some students ultimately achieve full independence, while others can do more than before with less assistance. Students also must learn to take responsibility for their behaviors. Teachers/specialists can help students navigate the community by teaching orientation, mobility, street directionality, how to use public transportation, or strategies for coping with getting lost or with timetable changes when traveling. They can also teach them to follow safety procedures. They can counsel them in choosing friends and provide behavioral procedures for choosing clothing and getting to school on time.

Problem-Solving Skills for Students with Disabilities

As much as some students with disabilities may want to be completely independent, some disabilities dictate that they will need help with some things at times. A crucial behavior included among problem-solving skills is having the judgment, willingness, and ability to ask for help when they really need it. Educators can help in one on one, small group, or whole class settings by initiating discussions wherein students identify situations they have experienced when they needed help; what they did; what they could have done instead; and discriminate situations where they could have succeeded independently from those where this was impossible. Some students can benefit by learning from the experiences their classmates share. Teachers/specialists can assess and teach student skills for identifying problems, give them practice in predicting the consequences of events/actions, develop various alternatives for responding to problems, and evaluate their relative effectiveness. They can also work with students individually and in groups on developing their own goals, plans, and solutions to problems.

Copyright © Mometrix Media. You have been licensed one copy of this document for personal use only. Any other reproduction or redistribution is strictly prohibited. All rights reserved.
This content is provided for test preparation purposes only and does not imply an endorsement by Mometrix of any particular political, scientific, or religious point of view.

SWPBS

School-wide positive behavioral support program (SWPBS) is not a practice, intervention, or curriculum per se. It is rather an operating framework for decision-making, toward the goal of assuring access for all students to the most effective possible teaching and behavioral interventions and practices. It guides a school's choice, integration, and application of evidence-based best practices to realize all students' best academic and behavioral outcomes. Six principles guiding SWPBS are: establishing a continuum of behavioral and academic supports and interventions based on science; utilizing real data for problem-solving and decision-making; organizing environments to prevent problem behaviors from occurring or developing; encouraging and teaching pro-social behaviors and skills; accountability and fidelity in implementing evidence-based behavioral practices; and universal screening and continuous monitoring of student performance and progress. Four interrelated elements of SWPBS are: data for making decisions; measurable outcomes, which data evaluate and support; practices backed by evidence they attain from the outcomes; and systems that support implementing the practices with effectiveness and efficiency.

Four integrated parts of SWPBS programs are data, practices, systems, and outcomes. The data educators collect about students' academic and social behaviors support the decisions they make about the academic and behavioral interventions and practices to use. The practices educators choose have science-based evidence of being effective for achieving the educational outcomes they desire. These practices support the desired student behaviors. The systems that educators establish support the most effective and efficient implementation of their chosen practices. These systems support implementation by supporting the behavior of the school personnel. The desired outcomes educators identify are observable and measurable, and the data they collect support these measurements. The students' outcomes in turn support the students' academic achievement and social competence. Well-implemented SWPBS makes learning environments less dangerous, exclusionary, aversive, and reactive, and more preventive, inclusive, engaging, and responsive. Disciplinary and classroom management issues like lateness, attendance, and antisocial behavior are addressed. Student behaviors needing more specialized interventions receive better support. And all students' academic motivation and performance are optimized.

School-wide positive behavioral support programs are typically divided into tiers along a continuum, based on how students respond behaviorally to intervention. In the first tier, all students in the school/system/district are given positive behavioral supports, such as giving positive rewards to reinforce exemplary and acceptable academic and social behaviors, which are implemented by all staff members in all school settings. This universal tier is known as primary prevention. The second tier of secondary prevention is for students whose behaviors do not respond to the behavioral supports given in the first tier, putting them at risk for disciplinary issues. These students are placed in a specialized group, where they receive more intensive behavioral measures. The third tier of tertiary prevention is for students identified as being at high risk of antisocial behaviors resulting in disciplinary problems and possible harm to themselves and/or others. These students receive individualized behavior management plans that are the most specialized and utilize the most intensive interventions.

COMMUNICATION AND EMERGENCY SITUATIONS

An important part of communicating with other people is being able to recognize emergency situations and respond timely and appropriately. This can be difficult for students with intellectual disabilities, behavior disorders, and other conditions. Among those who do not recognize an emergency situation, some will always require supervision, while others can be taught certain basics, such as the smell of smoke; the sight of fire, flooding, or a person needing emergency medical attention; and what to do, like calling 911. Some students with disabilities can recognize

Copyright © Mometrix Media. You have been licensed one copy of this document for personal use only. Any other reproduction or redistribution is strictly prohibited. All rights reserved.
This content is provided for test preparation purposes only and does not imply an endorsement by Mometrix of any particular political, scientific, or religious point of view.

emergency situations but may panic. Educators can use explicit, systematic instruction, including task analysis steps and behavioral shaping and chaining, to help them develop strongly entrenched procedures to follow. With enough practice, repetition, and reinforcement, many students with disabilities can implement these series of behaviors instead of panicking. Students with autism spectrum disorders often need explicit instruction in the meanings/purposes of social cues (like facial expressions, vocal intonations, gestures, body language, and verbal expressions) and how to respond appropriately.

Problem-Solving Procedure to Apply to Conflict Resolution

The teacher introduces the topic to students by explaining that where a conflict exists, a problem exists, and that having a way to think about and try to solve a problem helps. The teacher writes three steps on the board and goes over each step with the students: (1) Define the problem; (2) Brainstorm solutions; and (3) Choose a solution and act upon it. The teacher explains that before solving a problem, people must agree to work out the problem; that for problem-solving to work, they must agree not to call names, yell, or otherwise escalate the conflict. For step (1), the teacher encourages the students to define the problem in a way that does not place blame upon others. For step (2), the teacher encourages the students to think of as many possible solutions as they can. For step (3), the teacher advises the students that they should pick a "win-win" solution wherein all parties benefit and nobody loses.

To help younger and disabled students learn how to resolve conflicts, the teacher can first teach them a three-step problem-solving approach consisting of defining the problem, brainstorming solutions, and choosing and implementing a solution. The teacher then gives students a script for a "fight"/conflict and puppets if appropriate for the students, and then has some students volunteer to act out the conflict script. Then they review the problem-solving approach. Once students agree on one or more solutions, have the volunteer players act out their choice(s). Students who are able may then work in small groups to create and perform their own conflict resolution sketches for the class. The teacher then leads a class discussion, asking the students: (1) Which things in the sketches caused the conflict to escalate; (2) Which things people can say to each other to show they want to stop fighting and solve the problem; and (3) Whether any of the students have experienced similar conflicts in their own lives and how they resolved those conflicts.

ADLs and Task Analysis

Many of us take activities of daily living for granted. Because we have long ago learned to do them automatically, we do not realize how complex they actually are by involving many different steps. This complexity, however, can baffle special-needs students who have not achieved automaticity. Task analysis provides a solution by separating tasks into smaller, more manageable steps. Educators must also provide support, like going over each step with the student to ensure their understanding; helping with steps the student cannot do independently; answering student questions; and monitoring that they complete all steps correctly and in the right sequence. Daily life skills tasks can easily be connected with general education curriculum. For example, reading care instruction tags on clothing and directions on soap packages when doing laundry and discussing it with others connect with English. Measuring laundry soap, reading washing machine and dryer dials and numbers, sorting and counting clothes, and estimating washing and drying times connect with mathematics. This also applies to cooking, meal preparation, etc.

To function independently in the home or community, special-needs students must learn such ADLs as selecting clothes suitable for the day's weather and activities; doing grocery shopping for the week; performing personal hygiene like toileting, bathing, brushing teeth, etc.; organizing and doing household chores; managing money and paying bills; taking out garbage and retrieving

Copyright © Mometrix Media. You have been licensed one copy of this document for personal use only. Any other reproduction or redistribution is strictly prohibited. All rights reserved.
This content is provided for test preparation purposes only and does not imply an endorsement by Mometrix of any particular political, scientific, or religious point of view.

trash/recycling bins; cooking a simple meal; doing laundry; and others. Task analysis breaking a task down into individual steps is effective for special-needs students who otherwise have difficulty remembering all a task's parts and sequence. For example, doing laundry can be broken down into 10–12 steps. Before giving all steps to the student and supervising following them, the educator must follow these steps: Write down the steps, in chronological sequence. Assess what parts of steps the student can already do independently. Assess what steps/partial steps the student can do partly or with some adult assistance. Teach the student the steps that s/he cannot already do. Evaluate whether the instruction was effective for the student's learning.

Steps in Task Analysis for Laundry

(1.) Take the laundry hamper to the laundry room. (2.) Empty the hamper onto the table/floor. (3.) Sort laundry into colors and whites. (4.) Open the washing machine. (5.) Put one sorted pile (or as much of it as will fit easily) into the washer. (6.) Add laundry soap. (7.) Turn on the washer. (8.) Wait until the machine is done. (9.) Open the washer. (10.) Take the laundry out and look to make sure everything is clean. (11.) If not, remove soiled pieces and put them back into the washer for another cycle. (12.) Put laundry in the dryer.* (13.) Choose the right setting for the fabric type. (14.) If needed, set the length of drying time. (15.) Turn the dryer on. *[Alternative: Hang laundry on the clothesline to dry.] (16.) When laundry is dry, remove each piece from the dryer/clothesline. (17.) Fold each piece and put it into the hamper. (18.) Put away the clean laundry in the right closets, drawers, etc.

Picture Cards

Many special-needs students encounter difficulty processing information communicated verbally; initiating activities independently; maintaining attentional focus; and completing each step in a multiple-step task. When instructing special-needs students in ADLs, educators find a valuable resource in picture cards because these convey information visually instead of only verbally; they are naturally amenable to task analysis by using one picture card for each step in a task and arranging cards in the correct sequence; and they can be integrated into visual/graphic schedules, functional communication systems, and/or story strips. "Reminder strips" are short strips of picture cards that help students follow sequential steps when they cannot remember these without visual cues. For example, for hand-washing, a reminder strip placed above a sink can include individual pictures (with word captions) of turning on water, soap, lathering hands, turning off water, and drying hands on a towel, respectively. Many online resources offer printable cards, some designed for students to color themselves, which increases their engagement, enjoyment, and ownership in the learning process.

Adaptive Behavior Skills

To increase progress toward independent living, two of many important areas are time management and hygiene. While parents commonly wake their children, when they get older teaching them to use an alarm clock/clock-radio frees them from depending on parents. For students with ASDs, parents may need some trial-and-error experimentation with different loudness, sounds (e.g., beeps or buzzes or music, and music types) as many are hypersensitive to sensory stimuli. For those capable, advanced skills include setting the alarm independently and deciding when to set an alarm for by estimating the time they need. Parents/educators can also teach students to use a watch/clock to manage home/school task completion. Students having difficulty with numbers can benefit from graphic visual timers. Students also need to develop hygiene routines for bathing, using deodorant, grooming, and dressing. Many ASD students naturally have rigid behavior, find routines comforting, and are amenable to daily bathing/showering (which is easier long-term than every 2–3 days) and specific instructions, like washing each area four times.

Copyright © Mometrix Media. You have been licensed one copy of this document for personal use only. Any other reproduction or redistribution is strictly prohibited. All rights reserved.
This content is provided for test preparation purposes only and does not imply an endorsement by Mometrix of any particular political, scientific, or religious point of view.

Preparation for Independent Living

To prepare children with disabilities for more independent living as they grow up, parents and educators can start teaching young children responsibility for their belongings. For example, when young children bring their toys with them in the car or to others' homes, they can be taught a routine to find the toy before leaving, take it to the car, and bring it inside when arriving at home. As they get older, this routine can be transferred to backpacks, school supplies, digital devices, and phones. Adults can also teach young children to employ visual cues for remembering duties. For example, they can keep medications in specific locations as reminders to take them at the specified times. They can use Post-it notes on their backpacks reminding them to pack lunch and/or bring permission slips and completed assignments to school. Adults can begin teaching food preparation and how to make noncooked snacks and sandwiches to young children. As they grow, adults can teach them to follow recipes, safely utilize kitchen tools, and cook.

Adults can help many students with cognitive, behavioral, emotional/social, and mental health disabilities prepare for daily life. For example, for telephone skills, they can first teach young children to answer the telephone, and then take and deliver messages. As they grow, adults can help them progress with skills like calling 411 for phone numbers; calling stores in advance to ask if they have certain products in stock; calling restaurants to order takeout or delivered food; or calling technical support for help with computer issues. Adults can teach young children about walking to nearby neighborhood places; teach middle children about riding bicycles to destinations and taking public transportation when ready; and help adolescents and young adults learn to drive when appropriate. They can teach children as they grow to carry house keys, cell phones with important numbers, and money when leaving home; and personal safety, like judgment about hand-shaking versus hugging/kissing; protecting their personal information online and money in public; and what to do if followed/approached by strangers.

Career Awareness

When working with students with disabilities at the elementary school level, career development includes making students aware of workers in the community, and also helping them comprehend individual uniqueness, work's role in life, and fundamental knowledge about various jobs. Teachers can develop programs engaging students in activities involving adult workplaces and familiarize students with the kinds of social interactions they will experience after leaving school. Educators can also teach young students skills related to employment in the classroom, and then reinforce those skills in situations that expose them to workplace experience. Teachers can plan 1 to 3 hour field trips to visit different workplaces in their community. To prepare students, teachers can make them familiar with basic career information. After field trips, teachers can ask students questions like: What are the working environment and conditions? What abilities and skills do the jobs require? Do jobs observed primarily involve things, people, ideas, or information? Where/how can you learn skills for this occupation? Are you interested in this occupation? Why/why not?

To help prepare students with disabilities for futures in the workplace, educators can provide work experience in/around school. They can instruct them in doing laundry for the art room, gymnasium/pool, or lower grades' classrooms. Students can learn to sweep, vacuum, mop, wipe chairs and tables, and refill condiment containers in the cafeteria. Teachers can instruct students, sometimes with assistance from the custodial staff, in janitorial tasks like taking out garbage, dusting, cleaning, floor-waxing/buffing, painting, or refilling soap and paper towel dispensers. They can also enlist groundskeeper staff to help teach students seasonal outdoor tasks like weeding, mulching, mowing grass, and raking leaves. With the cooperation of office staff, teachers can instruct students in clerical tasks like preparing mail, making copies, filing, and data entry. Students can learn to help maintain school buses by vacuuming and washing. They can learn to restock

Copyright © Mometrix Media. You have been licensed one copy of this document for personal use only. Any other reproduction or redistribution is strictly prohibited. All rights reserved.
This content is provided for test preparation purposes only and does not imply an endorsement by Mometrix of any particular political, scientific, or religious point of view.

vending machines; collect and count the money and deliver it; recycle materials; or construct and paint scenery and run lights for school plays/assemblies.

School-to-Work Training

President Clinton signed the School to Work Opportunities Act of 1994 (Public Law 103-239) into law. This law is a joint initiative by the US Department of Education and Department of Labor. In transitions from school to work (STW), students with disabilities may need help with environmental accommodations; job accommodations; assistive technology devices; and additional supports for full participation in STW programs based in schools and/or communities. Key issues affecting success or failure in the workplace are related to social skills, for both nondisabled and disabled workers. In fact, 75 percent of job loss within the nondisabled population is attributed to poor social interactions. Disabled students also need good awareness of their own strengths and weaknesses to succeed at work, and skills for compensating for their deficits and making the most of their talents. Survey research with employers hiring disabled workers indicates that they want employees who are dependable, on time, can follow basic directions, and get along with their coworkers.

Some common STW curriculum subjects include employment-related functional academics; independent living skills; and interpersonal skills, since social skills are critical for nondisabled and disabled workers alike to get and keep jobs. Many opportunities connect school with work so students gain employment experience. Students can get unpaid/paid work experience through internships, structured for practically applying academic knowledge in jobs; job shadowing in one-day workplace visits and observing an employee in a specific job; or adult mentors, who serve as role models by communicating information about workplace norms, giving consistent, caring guidance and support, reviewing progress regularly, and establishing high expectations. Co-op programs combine technical and career classwork with part-time work during school years, with expectations for employers to provide and students to learn defined in training agreements. Community members visit schools on Career Days to share their experiences with interested students. Teachers can learn of academic job preparation through unpaid/paid workplace programs. Additional opportunities include apprenticeships, on-the-job training, field trips, class speakers, school-sponsored enterprises, and health care "clinicals."

Transition Planning and Indicator 13

Transition planning helps students with disabilities and their families consider students' lives after high school; identify long-term goals; tailor high school learning for acquiring skills and contacts they will need to meet those goals; and with allocation to local school districts of funding and services supporting transition processes. Students and adults invest in students' future well-being by planning for postsecondary life. The IDEA's Indicator 13 is a provision that students with disabilities age 16 and above must have IEPs including postsecondary transition plans. The US Department of Education's Office of Special Education Programs (OSEP) requires states to develop six-year State Performance Plans, based on about 20 indicators, and submit indicator data in Annual Performance Reports for Indicator 13 by February 2011. The National Secondary Transition Technical Assistance Center (NSTTAC) has developed the I-13 Checklist to aid state data collection. States may use their existing monitoring systems; however, this checklist can be used instead, or to evaluate those systems, or as a supplement, and is approved by the OSEP.

Postsecondary Transition Planning

The IDEA requires all students with disabilities to have postsecondary transition plans included in their IEPs when they are age 16 and older. When setting goals for students with disabilities to make transitions from school to work, job training and/or higher education, and community living, a few

Copyright © Mometrix Media. You have been licensed one copy of this document for personal use only. Any other reproduction or redistribution is strictly prohibited. All rights reserved.
This content is provided for test preparation purposes only and does not imply an endorsement by Mometrix of any particular political, scientific, or religious point of view.

general criteria include that the goals should reflect expectations that are both high and realistic for the student. These goals should also reflect an approach for some kind of forward progress rather than a dead-end situation. When establishing postsecondary goals, the goals and objectives may be of mixed character, reflecting the ability, endurance, and stamina levels of the individual student. The transition plan can and should include external supports as needed. Transition plans can begin with more general goals and incorporate more specific details as the student comes closer to graduation. These goals may change from one school year to the next. Changes can range from minor alterations to major differences, depending on the individual student and situation.

When planning postsecondary transitions for significantly disabled students, adults should consider whether the student is able to express his/her interests. If not, educators should obtain information from parents/caregivers for planning transitions. They should consider the student's special health care needs. They must account for any challenges or needs that keep the student from working outside of home. Transition planners must determine who can provide training and/or education to help the student's transitions. They must determine what the student can already do without others' assistance. And they must also consider what else the student could do if s/he had help from a habilitation training specialist, a job coach, a caregiver, or other service provider(s). Additional ideas for transition planning include connecting students and their families with other students who have similar disabilities and their families; identifying peer mentors for students; supplying the resources the student needs; and inviting others who can make valuable contributions to join the transition planning team.

Vocational assessment and planning: Employment preparation for disabled students contains the same essential components as for nondisabled students: assessing and establishing skills; exposure to career possibilities; and awareness of aptitudes and interests. However, greater and more individualized supports for these components are involved with disabled students. Successful school-to-work transition programs require transdisciplinary, comprehensive vocational assessment to identify student skills and needs by teachers, psychologists, counselors, and representatives from vocational rehabilitation and social services agencies and community mental health/intellectual disabilities departments as well as the students, parents, employers, and business organizations. Assessment should cover academic, daily living, personal, social, occupational, and vocational skills (including performance tests and situational assessments); career maturity; vocational interests; and vocational aptitudes. A number of standardized instruments are available for assessing the latter two. Three major goals for students to learn in school activities for vocational preparation are: understanding themselves, their abilities, interests, and values; understanding the world of work; and learning good decision-making skills. These enable informed, realistic work-related decisions, and are also the main elements of career maturity.

Copyright © Mometrix Media. You have been licensed one copy of this document for personal use only. Any other reproduction or redistribution is strictly prohibited. All rights reserved.
This content is provided for test preparation purposes only and does not imply an endorsement by Mometrix of any particular political, scientific, or religious point of view.

Professional Responsibilities

History of Disabilities and Special Education

Special education is a relatively new development in human history. Historically, people with disabilities received little or no education and were frequently placed into asylums or hospitals. The ancient Greek and Roman civilizations viewed disability as an evil omen, punishment from the gods. They viewed people as unable to change. Plato and Aristotle recommended euthanizing disabled infants. Cicero cited need for military superiority as reason to rid society of "defectives." The city/state took charge of soldiers disabled by combat. Due to ancient Greek and Roman philosophies, children born with disabilities were often drowned, "dashed against the rocks" as Homer described, thrown off cliffs, left to die on hilltops, chained up, or locked away. And fathers had the right to end a disabled child's life. In historical Christianity, while various physical ailments were treated as ritual impurities in the Old Testament, the New Testament shows Jesus healing the disabled, emphasizing their need for help and the goodness of helping them.

Middle Ages, the Renaissance, and the Enlightenment

In Medieval times (c. 500–1500 AD), society had a rigid caste system with royalty at the top, and no education for the masses. Some people with disabilities were exterminated; others were exploited as clowns, "fools," or servants. Generally, the disabled experienced ridicule for their differences. During the Renaissance (c. 1300–1700), when interest in knowledge was reborn, the Catholic Church made the disabled wards of the state, caring for them in isolation. They received more humane treatment, but initially no education. By the Enlightenment (c. 1650–1800), philosophers like John Locke believed all knowledge was acquired through the senses and all human beings were equal. Enlightenment philosophers believed humanity did not exist without education, increasing potential opportunities. During the Renaissance, in 1578, Spanish explorer Pedro Ponce de León first documented the education of royal deaf children. In 1760 during the Enlightenment, the French Abbé de L'Épée established the first institute for the deaf. In 1829 (the Regency era), Louis Braille invented his tactile reading/writing system for the blind.

Jean-Marc Gaspard Itard

Itard was a French doctor and educator, among the first to propose and prove special teaching methods could help educate children with disabilities. From 1801–1805, Itard used systematic instructional techniques to teach communication and daily living skills to a boy named Victor, discovered in the woods, seemingly without human rearing. Itard's work was made more famous by director/actor François Truffaut in his 1970 film *L'Enfant Sauvage* (*The Wild Child*). Itard's goals were to socialize Victor, improve his awareness of environmental stimuli, expose him to ideas, teach him to communicate, and advance his thinking from concrete/simple to abstract/complex. Some successes included increased regularity and control in Victor's eating, sleeping, and personal hygiene; improved senses of taste and touch; and increased range of interests. Victor learned to sequence objects and utter a few single-syllable words. However, he never developed connected speech or emotional attachments, and longed for his previous life. Some speculate Victor had intellectual disability or autism, which would also explain why he was likely abandoned at an early age.

Édouard Séguin

French doctor Séguin had studied with Jean-Marc Itard, who insisted that children with disabilities could learn via special instruction. In 1848 Séguin came to America, where he developed influential principles for educating intellectually disabled and other special-needs children. In his programs,

Copyright © Mometrix Media. You have been licensed one copy of this document for personal use only. Any other reproduction or redistribution is strictly prohibited. All rights reserved.
This content is provided for test preparation purposes only and does not imply an endorsement by Mometrix of any particular political, scientific, or religious point of view.

he emphasized presenting combined physical and intellectual tasks to help disabled children develop self-reliance and independence. He developed the physiological method, consisting of sensory training (particularly tactile) utilizing concrete materials, and also motor training, featuring movement from the simple to the complex, age-appropriate and functional activities, and activities involving both work and play. The major elements that made up the foundation of Séguin's educational philosophy and programs for instructing children with disabilities were: frequently changing activities; task analysis; discrimination between the senses and the intellect; sensory stimulation; physical education; and education with employment as an outcome. One can see from these elements the importance of Séguin's contributions, as these are all still prominent aspects of special education today over 150 years later.

Maria Montessori

Maria Montessori (1870–1952), an Italian doctor and educator, developed an entire philosophy of education with procedures based on its principles. Today there are many Montessori schools worldwide. While the Montessori method is intended for the general education of all children, it has many benefits for children with disabilities and inclusive education. It is based on the way children naturally learn through exploring and experience. Montessori aimed to enable children's optimal exploration and independent learning. To this end, she proposed the concept of the "prepared environment," a learning environment designed to facilitate this learning process. This environment features an uninterrupted continuum of learning experiences. Montessori schools divide classrooms into multiple-age groups: parent and infant for ages 0–3; preschool, ages 3–6; lower elementary, ages 6–9 and upper elementary, ages 9–12; and middle school, ages 12–14. However, this series of classrooms comprise a "flow" experience, wherein the child continuously constructs and builds upon his/her learning throughout the program. Classroom materials each isolate various single qualities/concepts like color, shape, or size.

20th Century

In the 1900s, the emphasis regarding disabilities was more biological than psychological or social. Hence many early pioneers of special education were both physicians and educators. Practitioners followed the medical model, and children with disabilities received institutional care. Between the 1900s and 1950s, laws made education compulsory, and educators created schools and classes for children who were blind, deaf, and mentally disabled. Following World War II, the special education system was established, with an organization parallel to the general education system. In the first of four main periods of special-needs education, children with blindness and deafness were most likely to receive instruction, while many children with other disabilities were still excluded from schools. In the second period, children with disabilities were segregated into homogeneous groups and received medical care and rehabilitation. The third period focused on normalizing and integrating the disabled into the community. In the fourth period, laws have mandated educational equality and inclusion rather than segregation in educational services for all children.

Characteristics of Special Education

Characteristics of "classic" special education include special settings; for example, segregated schools, classes, or resource rooms. Children are considered special, as evidenced by the way they are categorized, which determines their eligibility for special education and related services. "Classic" special education includes special teachers as well; whether they are trained and/or have experience or not, they are designated as special education teachers. Special education also includes therapists and other specialists trained to assess and remediate various conditions that qualify children for special education and related services. Special education traditionally involves a special teacher-student ratio: classes typically contain fewer students than general education classes, and more teachers per student. Another characteristic of special education is special

Copyright © Mometrix Media. You have been licensed one copy of this document for personal use only. Any other reproduction or redistribution is strictly prohibited. All rights reserved.
This content is provided for test preparation purposes only and does not imply an endorsement by Mometrix of any particular political, scientific, or religious point of view.

teaching methods and tools; for example, Braille for the blind, sign language for the deaf, or communication boards/books/systems/software for the nonverbal. Special education also includes special goals, such as integration into the social life of the community, and special programs for teaching needed skills not normally needed by other students.

Advantages and Disadvantages of Segregated Settings

In some cases, special schools and classes are still used today; however, in America and many other countries, laws mandate inclusive education for students with disabilities. Before this legislation, segregation was more the norm than the exception, yielding both advantages and disadvantages. Some advantages include: giving students with disabilities more chances of success; fostering cooperation instead of competition; being able to learn physical and social skills in accepting, understanding settings; staff with specialized training, specialized equipment, and specialized services; more opportunities to improve skills needed for greater participation in more inclusive settings; easier student access to individual attention; and more opportunities to meet other students with the same disability. Disadvantages include: developing "disabled" values, attitudes, and behaviors; lowered expectations in students, parents, and educators; resistance to transferring learned skills to regular settings; depriving disabled and nondisabled children of the benefits of interacting; less preparation for future living; greater lifelong expenses; more interactions with adults than with children; and performance standards separate from "normal" standards.

Medical Model vs. Social Model

Historically, early models of special education were based on the medical model of illness. As special education developed, the medical model came to be gradually replaced by the social model. Some key differences in these models are: The medical model viewed the child as defective, whereas the social model values the child as a unique individual. The medical model focused on diagnosing and labeling children by their disabilities; the social model strives to identify children's strengths and needs. The medical model focused on impairment; the social model focuses on identifying obstacles and developing solutions. The medical model dictated segregation and alternative services for the disabled; the social model dictates making necessary resources available to the disabled within inclusive settings. The medical model resulted in being excluded permanently from normal schools and society, or inclusion only if the individual eventually seemed sufficiently "normal" in appearance and behavior; the social model welcomes diversity. The medical model effected no social change; the social model causes society to evolve.

Overrepresentation of Certain Groups in Special Education

For the past 30 plus years, court cases and other legal actions have been filed against the special education system over excessive placement of culturally and linguistically diverse students in disability programs. ESL, low-income, African-American, Latino, and Native American students are commonly overrepresented, particularly in programs for LDs, mild intellectual disabilities, and emotional/behavioral disorders. The National Center for Culturally Responsive Educational Systems (NCCREST) advises parents to consult school administrators and/or parent advocates to investigate whether their school has this problem, because researchers disagree about formulae for assessing overrepresentation. However, they also offer one formula for calculating overrepresentation probability: using low-income students as an example, divide their number placed in (for example) LD classes by their total number in the school = percent placed in LD; calculate the same percentage of average income students in LD classes the same way; and divide the low-income percentage by the average income percentage. A result of + 1.0 indicates equal probabilities of special education placement; > 1.0 indicates greater placement probability for lower income students.

Copyright © Mometrix Media. You have been licensed one copy of this document for personal use only. Any other reproduction or redistribution is strictly prohibited. All rights reserved.
This content is provided for test preparation purposes only and does not imply an endorsement by Mometrix of any particular political, scientific, or religious point of view.

Inclusion

Internationally, in 1948, the Universal Declaration of Human Rights addressed rights to inclusive education, as did the UN Convention on the Rights of the Child in 1989. In 1990, the World Declaration for Education for All addressed inclusion. In 1993, the Standard Rules on the Equalization of Opportunities for Persons with Disability established rights of disabled people to equal opportunities in education and employment. In 1994, UNESCO (the United Nations Educational, Scientific, and Cultural Organization) issued the Salamanca Statement and Framework for Action on every child's basic rights to education, stating that educational systems and programs should address children's diversities; special-needs students require adaptations enabling regular school access; and inclusive regular schools most effectively fight and prevent discrimination and make society inclusive. Significant US laws include Section 504 of the 1973 Rehabilitation Act; the Education for all Handicapped Children Act (EHA) (1975/1986); the Americans with Disabilities Act (ADA, 1990); the Individuals with Disabilities Education Act (IDEA, 1997/2004); and the No Child Left Behind (NCLB, 2001) Act.

Recent and Current Trends Related to Technology, Inclusion, and Early Intervention

Technological progress has afforded increased opportunities for both students and teachers in special education. Computer software programs enable students with speech and language and visual disabilities to convert text to speech; hearing-impaired students to convert speech to text; and ESL students to read translations in their native languages. Websites offer students more independent schoolwork at their own pace; multimodal presentations for LD students; and the ability for ADHD students to alternate among shorter units and topics. Students with auditory processing difficulties, and teachers needing more instructional materials, can access more graphic/visual stimuli online. The Internet also facilitates student/parent/teacher access to advocates, support groups, and organizations. Trends are increasingly toward inclusion, with more students mainstreamed than ever. Special classes and schools exist when needs require/parents prefer, but the IDEA's LRE requirement moves more students into regular education classes/curricula/schools. Whereas learning disabilities were previously identified and services recommended in upper-elementary grades or later, today screening, assessment, identification, and intervention are advised by early childhood or even earlier.

Behavior Management

The Council for Exceptional Children's Code of Ethics states this principle: "Special education professionals participate with other professionals and...parents in an interdisciplinary effort in the management of behavior." No one approach works with all students in all situations. While classroom management interventions may be ideally designed and implemented, not addressing individual children's needs and wants limits their effects. Hence one/several students in a class/setting may need behavior management strategies targeting specific behaviors. Cognitive interventions can affect emotional behaviors and psychomotor interventions can influence cognitive and affective development. Educators, parents, and others frequently ask about changing individual and group student behaviors; whether to punish or ignore behaviors; whether to discuss behaviors with students; and whether interventions are ethical, harmful, or effective. CEC suggests an educator activity like the following. Small groups list target behaviors and individual/group interventions, discussing whether these treat students with dignity, teach new skills, and support/need environmental analysis; whether student responses are clear to everybody, including students; whether educators respond sequentially to target behaviors (e.g., the second time a behavior occurs).

Copyright © Mometrix Media. You have been licensed one copy of this document for personal use only. Any other reproduction or redistribution is strictly prohibited. All rights reserved.
This content is provided for test preparation purposes only and does not imply an endorsement by Mometrix of any particular political, scientific, or religious point of view.

Classroom Management and Behavior Management

According to researchers (e.g., Smith & Rivera, 1995), to establish/maintain classroom order, teachers should develop positive atmospheres and foundations of positive learning environments; use preventive techniques; develop collaboration with parents and other professionals around disciplinary issues; make sure interventions are appropriate to the problems they address; and regularly evaluate student progress. The goal of behavior management strategies is self-discipline, defined as gaining control over one's behavior in varied situations with various groups and individuals. Some ethical concerns include questions like these: Who decides who will manage behavior and whose behavior will be managed? How can others control behavior managers? Which interventions will be used, and who decides on accepted interventions? For what goals/purposes will interventions be implemented? Are/should children be free to make choices? Are student actions observable, measurable, repeated, and congruent with behavioral principles? In schools: Can externals—educators, peers, parents—change student behavior? Who decides which/whose behaviors to change? What interventions are used in classrooms? And who monitors them?

Under its ethical principle regarding behavior management, the Council for Exceptional Children (CEC) includes the following: (1) Professionals must use only behavioral procedures and disciplinary techniques they have been told to use, and that do not compromise individual student dignity or exceptional students' fundamental human rights (e.g., corporal punishment). (2) Professionals must specify clearly in the student's IEP any goals and objectives related to behavior management. (3) Professionals must comply with rules, statutes, and policies of state and local agencies regarding appropriately applying behavioral and disciplinary practices. (4) When they perceive a coworker's behavior as detrimental to special education students, professionals must take sufficient measures for preventing, discouraging, and intervening with those actions. (4) Professionals must avoid using aversive methods, unless repeated uses of other techniques were ineffective, and then only after consulting with parents and applicable agency officials.

Educators should always explore alternate behavioral interventions before considering any aversive methods. When considering/planning behavioral interventions, educators should first explore any possible injury or side effects these could cause. Before arranging contingencies to apply to student behaviors, educators should discern whether the student understands the contingency. Anyone implementing any behavioral intervention with a student must both have sufficient training in the procedures and feel comfortable applying the intervention. Interventions should be backed by empirical evidence of their effectiveness; be consistent with student programs and parental input; and have written informed parental consent. Behavioral intervention programs must be closely monitored and thoroughly documented. Procedures of legal due process and committee reviews should be followed. Behavioral interventions/programs should comply with the IDEA's Least Restrictive Environment requirement. Interventions should be commensurate with relative seriousness of the behavior; afford student opportunity to succeed; respect individual student worth and dignity; be fair; and address the principle of normalization (disabled students have rights to lives as close to normal as possible).

Legal Requirements of School Districts and Legal Rights of Parents

Under current federal laws, all public school districts are required to invite parental participation in meetings regarding the evaluation, identification, and placement of their children in special education; notify parents in writing of any intentions to identify/assess/place their child in special education or change their identification/assessment/placement; notify parents in native languages/formats they understand; inform parents of resources available to help them understand written school notifications; and give parents copies of their legal rights and responsibilities and all procedural safeguards. Parents have the right to give written consent for referral, evaluation, re-

Copyright © Mometrix Media. You have been licensed one copy of this document for personal use only. Any other reproduction or redistribution is strictly prohibited. All rights reserved.
This content is provided for test preparation purposes only and does not imply an endorsement by Mometrix of any particular political, scientific, or religious point of view.

evaluation, and placement in special education of their children; review all educational records regarding these; have interpreters supplied when they are not native English speakers; contribute input to all assessments, conversations, and decisions, initially and/or subsequently; request independent evaluations not paid by them if they disagree with district evaluation/diagnosis; participate in eligibility determination and placement; receive copies of evaluations, reports, and eligibility determination documents; and receive regular progress reports during their children's special education program placement.

Children's Rights During Behavior Management Process

According to the Council for Exceptional Children, children have rights in the areas of normalization, fairness, and respect. The principle of normalization means that a person with a disability has the right to develop a life that is as close as possible to that of normal persons. The principle of fairness includes not only basic fairness, but also the due process of law. Educators must determine whether a specific intervention they choose for modifying a student's behavior is fair to the student as an individual. The principle of respect means the student has the right to be treated as a human being rather than a statistic or an animal. Educators must measure any intervention in light of this principle. For example, physical or psychological punishment, segregation or isolation, medication, shock, restraints, or other punishments usually violate this principle. Ethics encompassing these principles dictate that in behavior management procedures, the means do NOT justify the end unless the principles of normalization, fairness, and respect have been met.

Confidentiality

The National Association of Special Education Teachers (NASET)'s Code of Ethics contains six principles. Principle 5 states: "NASET Members collaborate with parents of children with special needs and community, building trust and respecting confidentiality." Under this principle, subsection 5-E states, "NASET Members respect the private nature of the special knowledge they have about children and their families and use that knowledge only in the students' best interests." (2006/2007, NASET) The Family Educational Rights and Privacy Act (FERPA, 1974, aka Buckley Amendment) is the primary legislation delimiting accessibility and disclosure of student records. Privacy regarding student participation in evaluation, analysis, and surveys is defined by the Grassley Amendment (1994) to the Goals 2000: Educate America Act of 1994. Records of student drug and alcohol treatment kept by any entity receiving federal funding have protection under the Drug Abuse Office and Treatment Act (1976). In addition to these laws, the Individuals with Disabilities Education Act (IDEA, 1997/2004) protects the confidentiality of records for students receiving special education and related services.

Culturally and Linguistically Diverse Students

School's Climate and Philosophy

A school's principal should advocate strongly for the well-being and interests of culturally and linguistically diverse students receiving special education and related services. Parents and teachers should consider how the principal shows her/his commitment in this respect. A school's curriculum should reflect the viewpoints, contributions, and experiences of diverse linguistic and ethnic groups. Parents should consider whether a school's principal and staff blame diverse students or their families for different educational performance levels, and whether schools pressure diverse families to embrace school values, or work to incorporate cultural and language differences into their instructional programs. It is important to look for ways in which school administrators and staff demonstrate respect for language and cultural differences. Parents will want to consider whether the environment of a given school is orderly and safe for their children.

Copyright © Mometrix Media. You have been licensed one copy of this document for personal use only. Any other reproduction or redistribution is strictly prohibited. All rights reserved.
This content is provided for test preparation purposes only and does not imply an endorsement by Mometrix of any particular political, scientific, or religious point of view.

Additionally, a school should demonstrate high expectations and provide sufficient achievable curricular challenges, both supported by evidence, for all of its students.

Approaches to Prevent Unnecessary Referrals to Special Education

A school should recognize and incorporate cultural and linguistic differences in their practices related to assessment, curriculum planning and design, and instruction. Considering the demographics of American society today, all/most schools should have ESL programs. Classroom instruction and other school functions should include languages other than English. Schools should have support systems in addition to special education, such as tutoring programs, teacher assistance teams, and bilingual education programs. Schools should collaborate with their communities in established programs. They should also support their teachers via professional development offerings that respond to needs expressed by faculty members and continuing collaboration and consultation of teachers with other professionals. Educators should build upon students' existing knowledge and use interactive discourse to promote both fundamental and higher order student skills for reading, math, and writing. Schools should systematically and continually evaluate student progress and the quality of their programs. Decision-making should include all relevant stakeholders. School educators should include cooperative learning methods and thematic instructional techniques in their teaching.

Assessment

The assessment stage is when professionals collect data used to determine or rule out disability; therefore, parents and cultural diversity experts should be included in the assessment team. Assessment plans should always include multiple instruments and settings to be comprehensive and reflect multiple perspectives and approaches. How student difficulties are addressed and what consequences result across various settings should also be considered. Suspected disabilities in ELLs should be assessed in a student's dominant language. Educators should gather data on student proficiency and educational achievement in both his/her first language and English. Assessment teams must obtain parental perceptions, beliefs, values, and expectations about children's learning/behavioral challenges. Schools should avoid interpreters and test translations. However, if these are unavoidable, they should document interpreter skills; ensure multiple formal and informal assessments and information sources; use peers from normative groups; and, if tests are invalidated, seek performance patterns rather than absolute scores. With behavioral referrals, educators should consider obtaining more information to corroborate interpretations of projective instruments, which can be subjective.

Eligibility Determination and Placement

Parents of culturally and linguistically diverse backgrounds should become involved in all stages of the special education process if their children are referred. In addition to being included on referral and assessment teams, parents as well as cultural diversity experts should be included in decision-making for eligibility determination and placement. This team should consider whether a student's difficulties are caused by a possible disability, cultural/social differences, or both. Immigration, switching schools, and school absences should be considered. Evidence of different sources of student difficulty should be provided. If a student is identified with a disability, parents should determine whether the school has specific plans for reviewing the student's circumstances in the future, determining whether the student might be reclassified. If a student is determined eligible for special education, parents should know whether team members work for placement in the least restrictive environment and seek proof/evidence of such efforts. They should find out if students with the same disability type and age are placed in similar programs and why..

Copyright © Mometrix Media. You have been licensed one copy of this document for personal use only. Any other reproduction or redistribution is strictly prohibited. All rights reserved.
This content is provided for test preparation purposes only and does not imply an endorsement by Mometrix of any particular political, scientific, or religious point of view.

Special Education Referral Process

Because diverse students are frequently overrepresented in special education referrals, their parents should be included on referral teams, as well as persons with expertise regarding cultural diversity. Educators should review these factors before recommending comprehensive evaluations: the school and classroom climate; all attempts at pre-referral intervention and their results; any temporary problems in the classroom, home, and/or community; educator effort in building on students' cultural experiences and knowledge and their strengths; and observations by parents when possible, and by qualified others with knowledge of cultural differences, of the student's current classroom—particularly if the referral is for behavior management, as these problems can be influenced by teacher behavior management approaches. In addition, it is only appropriate to refer ESL/ELL students if: students have good communication skills in their native languages but are behind peers in English, and instructional adaptations have been implemented; students are academically proficient in English, receive effective reading instruction, and still demonstrate significant reading problems; and/or effective ESL or bilingual instruction do not improve academic English-language skills.

Collaboration Between Special Educators and General Educators

As all teachers have various strengths and needs, special educators should share these. General educators are likely less familiar with specialized resources for matching practices to student skill levels when these are far beneath grade level; special educators are likely less acquainted with the richness of grade-level projects and activities. Both types of teachers can pool their knowledge of proactive/preventive and disciplinary techniques, and two pairs of eyes can better prevent misbehavior and identify desirable behavior to reinforce. General educators have training in using and instructing students with many kinds of software; special educators contribute working familiarity with assistive technology. For routine planning, special and general educators can help each other develop simple student routines. While structure and content often easily combine in general education, special-needs students must learn how assignment directions are structured before addressing assignment contents. Teachers can use tracing/matching routines to plan independent student activities. Praise motivates teachers as well as students: collaborating special and general educators should regularly praise each other's successes verbally.

When collaborating, teachers must schedule *at least* one weekly planning session, even if it must be after school. Co-teachers will fail through unmet expectations and lack of communication without such planning. As in any relationship, co-teachers do not know everything about one another. They must share their ideas and experiences, not only to succeed in teaching their students, but to understand their own teaching and learning processes and to experience job satisfaction. Teacher collaboration processes will undergo changes, just as students discover new concepts over time through their teachers and their instructional methods. While these changes mean that co-teachers and students alike will encounter surprises and adjustments, they also mean that teachers will develop better ways of meeting student needs. Collaboration also affords teachers new perspectives. They can take advantage of these by making focused observations and asking reflective questions whenever not directly occupied in instructional delivery. Taking brief but specific notes helps co-teachers discuss observations later, troubleshoot/problem-solve, fine-tune instruction, and communicate student successes.

Regardless of which co-teacher is leading a lesson/activity at the time, both should be actively interacting with students, which includes physical movement: one's viewpoint is narrowed when sitting at one's desk/in a classroom corner, whereas moving about enables a global view. Co-teachers should determine shared organizational goals and periodically review these. During the school year, considering organization is often sacrificed under time pressures; however, small

Copyright © Mometrix Media. You have been licensed one copy of this document for personal use only. Any other reproduction or redistribution is strictly prohibited. All rights reserved.
This content is provided for test preparation purposes only and does not imply an endorsement by Mometrix of any particular political, scientific, or religious point of view.

enhancements in organization can have major influences. Co-teachers can examine their total classroom environment for smooth flow of activities and how well students stay organized. Special educators can contribute techniques to establish regular external structures for students with deficits in executive functioning who do not generate such structure internally. They can help general education teachers with monitoring students and supporting their organizational needs through simple structures incorporating task analysis for following step-by-step routines, visual cues, and instruction in self-monitoring routines. Co-teachers should reflect on their entire process, analyze it, and respond. They can experiment with co-teaching methods they could not use individually.

Curriculum and Data Collection

Many special educators, such as special education resource teachers, often teach students in multiple grades. To support their students' various educational needs, the special education teacher must know the general education curriculum. When this teacher works with multiple grade levels, s/he has to know multiple different curricula. This teacher must also collaborate with all students' general classroom teachers to ensure s/he supports what they teach. This entails both making time and being organized to speak with each teacher individually. Special education teachers must also provide data for each student, to document instruction that implements the student's IEP and document their reports of student success or difficulty in each area. They must monitor data collection, analyze data, and adjust instruction accordingly. They need the cooperation of general education teachers in collecting data when they are not in the general classrooms with students. While parents/others may volunteer to help collect data, special education confidentiality laws can prohibit volunteers without permission from the parents of every student in class.

Communicating and Collaborating with Community Agencies

When special education students have already had interactions with some government departments like the juvenile justice system, the mental health system, or the department of social services, those agencies may initiate contact with schools/teachers. In other cases, educators may need to contact them. Community agencies dedicated to children with disabilities and all those working with/for them serve as liaisons/links to public and private schools and government departments, local officials, and legislators. Some community agencies offer services like direct representation; educators can invite them to IEP meetings and due process mediations and hearings on behalf of disabled students and their families to ensure effective advocacy, information, and support. Teachers can help get parents training on their rights and special education services from community agencies. Community agencies can provide professional educators and families with consultations on technical assistance for students with disabilities. If parents and school districts disagree, educators can enlist mediation services from some community agencies to prevent escalation into court cases.

Working with Other Professionals, Teaching Aides, Assistants, and Paraprofessionals

When educational research investigates high turnover rates among special educators, some researchers have thought the voluminous paperwork in special education was responsible, only to hear from some special education teachers that they attribute turnover more to being appreciated less than general education teachers. Special education teachers often must coordinate their schedules with art teachers, music teachers, physical education teachers, and 10–20 other teachers, and also show consideration to physical therapists, occupational therapists, and speech-language pathologists, as well as accounting for lunch and recess when making resource schedules. Even minor changes in general education teachers' schedules can alter the special education teacher's whole day or week. Most special education teachers are enormously grateful to their aides,

Copyright © Mometrix Media. You have been licensed one copy of this document for personal use only. Any other reproduction or redistribution is strictly prohibited. All rights reserved.
This content is provided for test preparation purposes only and does not imply an endorsement by Mometrix of any particular political, scientific, or religious point of view.

assistants, and paraprofessionals; however, the reality is they must also devote significantly more time and effort to train them and create daily schedules for them. A teacher's aide differing in opinion from the teacher's, especially if the aide is older/more experienced than the teacher, presents an additional challenge to teamwork, for which the teacher is responsible.

STANDARDS FOR CREDENTIALS AND EMPLOYMENT OF SPECIAL EDUCATION PROFESSIONALS

Some of the Council for Exceptional Children practice standards for special education professionals in credentials and employment include: represent oneself accurately, legally, and ethically regarding their expertise and knowledge to prospective employers; assure that those representing themselves and/or practicing as special education administrators, teachers, and related service providers have the qualifications of professional credentials; operate within their limits of professional skills and knowledge, and appropriately seek consultation and/or support from sources outside themselves as necessary; comply with contractual terms of employment; comply with policies and contracts of local education agencies for notifying them when terminating their positions; advocate for supportive and suitable educational conditions, and for staffing resources sufficient to keep absences of support staff or substitute teachers from causing special education services to be denied; and get professional help for personal problems affecting work performance.

In addition to nine others, the CEC (Council for Exceptional Children) identifies standards for special education professionals that include: documenting and reporting objectively any deficits in resources, and offering solutions for these to their supervisors/administrators; evaluating employment applicants and grievances objectively, without discrimination; utilizing established procedures to resolve professional workplace problems; expecting their responsibilities to be conveyed to coworkers, and assuring their understanding and respect of those responsibilities; requesting clear written statements of their employment conditions, duties, and responsibilities; participating actively in planning, management, and evaluation of special education programs and general education programs, and in associated policy development; expecting sufficient support and supervision for special education professionals, and for programs delivered by qualified professionals in special education; and expecting there to be clearly defined chains of accountability and responsibility regarding the supervision and administration of professionals in special education.

PROFESSIONAL DEVELOPMENT

Special education professionals cannot allow their training, knowledge, and expertise to remain at the same level throughout their working lives as when they received their degrees and certification and began working. They must continually update, improve, and expand their skills, both to remain current in this dynamic, changing profession and to grow as educators. Special education professionals acquire and apply knowledge about developmental levels and readiness for various instructional interventions. They learn about research evidence-based instructional strategies, and then apply these for teaching fundamental skills in literacy and numeracy to students with special needs. They know how to individualize their instruction for each student, and they continue to learn new strategies and techniques to improve this individualization process. They assess student progress on an ongoing basis and refine their assessment techniques to increase their accuracy and applications to adjustments and modifications in their instructional approaches. They make use of data and continually inform themselves of newer data from emergent research to apply to their problem-solving endeavors. They prepare students to become independent.

In the area of professional development, the Council for Exceptional Children (CEC) has standards that include: systematically keeping individualized plans for their own professional development, designing these to increase their own skills, knowledge, and cultural competence to sustain high

Copyright © Mometrix Media. You have been licensed one copy of this document for personal use only. Any other reproduction or redistribution is strictly prohibited. All rights reserved.
This content is provided for test preparation purposes only and does not imply an endorsement by Mometrix of any particular political, scientific, or religious point of view.

competency levels; keeping current in their knowledge of laws, policies, and procedures related to their practices; systematically and objectively evaluating themselves, their coworkers, and their programs and services to enhance their professional performance continually; advocating for effective, schoolwide professional development and individual professional development plans being provided by their employing agencies; participating in supervised, systematic field experiences for special education professional candidates as a part of their educator preparation degree and certification programs; and functioning as mentors for other special educators in whichever times, places, and circumstances that their doing so is appropriate.

A number of organizations offer professional development courses. For example, the National Association of Special Education Teachers (NASET) has many classes. Professionals can learn more about modifications for alternative assessments; the annual and triennial review processes; assistive technologies for students with disabilities; ADHD, anxiety disorders, autism, pervasive developmental disorders, bipolar disorder, depression, Down syndrome, eating disorders, emotional disturbances, epilepsy, LDs, intellectual disabilities, orthopedic impairments, multiple disabilities, PTSD, Rett syndrome, schizophrenia, speech-language disorders, spina bifida, Tourette syndrome, traumatic brain injuries, blindness and visual impairments, deafness and hearing impairments, and deaf-blindness; auditory processing disorders; developmental and psychological disorders in special education; criteria for eligibility determination for special education services related to each disability; educational implications of some disorders; factors influencing curriculum for special-needs students; identification of high-risk students in classrooms; developing, writing, implementing, reviewing, and modifying IEPs; medications; services related to special education; team transitional planning; and helping students cope with disasters and violence.

Self-Assessments

Many school districts and systems have created self-assessment rubrics or instruments for special educators. These instruments generally list specific standards for an array of required skills and knowledge, including operational definitions that describe what knowledge, skills, and behaviors the special educator should demonstrate. These descriptions are accompanied by incremental rating scales. The educator reads each competency and checks a box corresponding to whether s/he thinks s/he, for example, models it, adjusts upon reflecting, and is a resource for others (the highest score); or works independently to apply the competency across settings and self-initiates planning (the second highest); applies the competency with support and shows emerging self-initiation of planning (the middle score); understands and tries to apply the competency, and uses resources for improving his/her teaching (the second lowest); or is aware of the competency but has no experience in and/or does not demonstrate it (the lowest score). Another example states competence areas for self-rating as highly effective, effective, minimally effective, or ineffective.

Strategies to Reflect on Effectiveness of Work

Research finds viewing video recordings of their teaching practices in combination with collaborative professional development courses and activities helps teachers enhance and change their practices. In one pilot study (Osipova, et al, 2011) teachers viewed many video recordings of themselves teaching throughout the school year. They self-reflected, noting what they did effectively, generating suggestions for future teaching, and rating their instruction. The researchers found this process altered teachers' initial self-reflections overestimating their practices to more critical self-examinations. It changed teachers' self-reflection comments, vague at first, to more specific descriptions. Teachers particularly realized they attended to certain students and not others. Because not all teachers apply what they learn in professional development to their classroom practices, researchers find guided/coached critical self-reflection instrumental for

Copyright © Mometrix Media. You have been licensed one copy of this document for personal use only. Any other reproduction or redistribution is strictly prohibited. All rights reserved.
This content is provided for test preparation purposes only and does not imply an endorsement by Mometrix of any particular political, scientific, or religious point of view.

changing teacher beliefs about learning and teaching, which are frequently unspoken and even unconscious. Teachers are more likely to change their practices once they change their beliefs, and also when they view themselves as learners. Video self-reflection affords self-analyses with multiple foci, and also repeated self-analyses of teaching practices.

Copyright © Mometrix Media. You have been licensed one copy of this document for personal use only. Any other reproduction or redistribution is strictly prohibited. All rights reserved.
This content is provided for test preparation purposes only and does not imply an endorsement by Mometrix of any particular political, scientific, or religious point of view.

TExES Practice Test

Want to take this practice test in an online interactive format?
Check out the online resources page, which includes interactive practice questions and much more: **mometrix.com/resources719/texeseddiag253**

1. Norm-referenced tests:

a. Evaluate students' scores by comparing them to scores of a group of other test-takers
b. Evaluate a student's scores by referencing them to a set standard or criterion
c. Are informal assessments
d. Include statewide standardized assessments

2. The following teaching strategies all promote reading proficiency. Which one is more related to practice than to motivation?

a. Providing choices in the reading materials for students
b. Finding ways to make reading meaningful to students
c. Finding ways to make reading fun for students
d. Providing the students with many opportunities to read

3. Which law is most concerned that a student's special education folder and files be kept confidential?

a. Family Educational Rights and Privacy Act (FERPA)
b. Individuals with Disabilities Act (IDEA)
c. The Education for All Handicapped Children Act of 1975
d. Health Insurance Portability and Accountability Act of 1996 (HIPAA)

4. Which organization grants certifications to Educational Diagnosticians?

a. The State Board for Educator Certification
b. The Texas Education Agency
c. Texas Educational Diagnostician's Association
d. The college from which the diagnostician graduated grants the certifications.

5. In a student's IEP, modifications and/or accommodations may be listed. A modification is:

a. Any change to the instructional methods utilized by the student's teachers
b. A change to what or how much is being taught in the TEKS content
c. A change in the tools used to teach, such as including graphic organizers
d. Any change in who is teaching the TEKS content, such as a teacher's aide

6. If a student is identified as having a learning disability in math, allowing the student to use a calculator in math would be considered:

a. An accommodation
b. A modification
c. Cheating
d. Something which is only available to students in special education

Copyright © Mometrix Media. You have been licensed one copy of this document for personal use only. Any other reproduction or redistribution is strictly prohibited. All rights reserved.
This content is provided for test preparation purposes only and does not imply an endorsement by Mometrix of any particular political, scientific, or religious point of view.

7. The goals of emphasizing the need for Response to Intervention (RtI) in No Child Left Behind Act of 2001 and IDEA 2004 include all of the following except:

a. Provide early interventions
b. Ensure that low achievement is not the result of poor instruction
c. Adjust interventions continually based on progress
d. Student progression through the multi-tiers of the RtI system in place of a referral

8. According to the Federal IDEA guidelines, the student must be invited to ARD meetings at least:

a. By age 15
b. By age 16
c. By age 17
d. By age 18

9. When administering assessments to students, what should the educational diagnostician keep in mind with regard to issues of diversity?

a. All students are given the same assessments regardless of diversity issues, such as the student's ethnicity, cultural background and socioeconomic status.
b. All assessments commonly used are valid and reliable for all students, regardless of diversity issues.
c. The diagnostician needs to make sure that each assessment given to a student is valid and reliable for that particular student's subgroups, whether it is cultural, socioeconomic, language, or ethnicity.
d. Tests may be appropriate even if they weren't developed using the student's subgroup.

10. When standardizing tests, it is important to:

a. Administer the test to the test takers while they are the most comfortable
b. Give the test to whoever would like to take it to help out the field and increase sample size
c. Score and interpret the data to use as a context for future test takers of the same test
d. Define the representative sample and testing conditions independently each time the test is administered

11. A student, Klara, is in special education, and her evaluation and corroboration by teachers and her parents indicate that she has a handwriting disability. To address this issue what would be an appropriate accommodation/modification to include in Klara's IEP?

a. Allow her type or dictate to a scribe all of her assignments/tests/papers rather than handwrite them
b. Allow her to not have to complete any assignments which require her to handwrite in class
c. Allow her to opt-out of writing assignments but use a scribe with math assignments
d. Allow her to work with other students at all times to complete assignments

12. The ARD committee can decide which of the following services are needed except:

a. Enabling the child to advance appropriately toward attaining his/her annual goals
b. Being involved and make progress in the general curriculum
c. Being educated with non-disabled peers, as appropriate
d. Initial program placement

Copyright © Mometrix Media. You have been licensed one copy of this document for personal use only. Any other reproduction or redistribution is strictly prohibited. All rights reserved.
This content is provided for test preparation purposes only and does not imply an endorsement by Mometrix of any particular political, scientific, or religious point of view.

13. A child, who has been diagnosed by the family doctor as having Asperger's Syndrome, is assessed by the educational diagnostician and an ARD is held. If the ARD committee decides that the child is eligible for special education services due to the effects of Asperger's Syndrome, under which IDEA disability category will the child meet eligibility?

a. Other Health Impairment
b. Emotional Disturbance
c. Autism
d. Asperger's Syndrome

14. John is a 12th grade student in special education who has just turned 18. John has never felt comfortable in special education and has not thought that it was needed in order for him to be successful in school. He decides when he turns 18 to request to be removed from special education, although the rest of the ARD committee and his parents disagree with his decision. What must the school do legally?

a. Remove John from special education since he is now a legal adult and his consent must be obtained to receive special education services.
b. The ARD committee still has the final say, and the vote to remove him must be unanimous.
c. The parents still have final say since the student is living with them and counted as a dependent on their tax records.
d. If the ARD committee and John's parents agree, they can appeal John's decision to a higher authority in order to override his request to be removed from special education services

15. A student's score on an assessment will equal their true score plus:

a. Their teacher's thoughts on what the student's score should be
b. Error
c. Standard deviation
d. The student's percentile rank

16. All educational diagnosticians are required to complete at least how many clock hours of Continuing Professional Education (CPE) during each five-year renewal period?

a. 100
b. 200
c. 300
d. 400

17. The reason parents must be given the Procedural Safeguards is to:

a. Enhance parents' ability to effectively participate in decision-making processes involving the education of their children
b. Ensure that the school is not sued
c. Ensure that parents understand how eligibility for each disability category is determined
d. Reduce the number of questions which parents may ask the ARD committee

18. Who of the following would not be an appropriate ARD committee member?

a. A current general education teacher
b. A current special education teacher
c. A special education teacher from the previous year
d. A representative of the school district

Copyright © Mometrix Media. You have been licensed one copy of this document for personal use only. Any other reproduction or redistribution is strictly prohibited. All rights reserved.
This content is provided for test preparation purposes only and does not imply an endorsement by Mometrix of any particular political, scientific, or religious point of view.

19. Which of the following is the best example of an evidence-based assessment of a student's basic writing skills?

a. Test of Written Language (TOWL)
b. Informal observation by teacher
c. A classroom writing inventory
d. A rubric-based assessment

20. The difference between disciplinary rules and ethical considerations for a diagnostician are:

a. Disciplinary rules mean that the practitioner may face disciplinary action if the rules are not followed.
b. It is up to the practitioner to decide if ethical considerations should or should not be followed.
c. Disciplinary rules and ethical considerations are essentially the same.
d. It is impossible to break a disciplinary rule and be reinstated, but there is a process for being reinstated after an ethical violation

21. Which of the following statements is false regarding diversity issues in evaluation?

a. Students should always be tested in English since it is the language that they are held accountable to learn in school.
b. When gathering information from parents who do not speak English, it is important to have an interpreter who is both fluent in the parents' native language, but also understands the basic tenets of special education. This will aid in translation accuracy, as well assurance that the guidelines of special education are not breached.
c. When interviewing/speaking with students or parents from a different culture, it is important to be aware of the possible miscommunications which may occur as the result of various factors, such as eye contact. Meanings attached to different behaviors may vary from culture to culture.
d. Students who are not fluent in English will also have difficulty in other subject areas, such as math or history, as a result of difficulty reading course material and having trouble interpreting what is expected of them.

22. What is the one exception to qualifying for the disability category of Multiple Disabilities -- when a student has two or more qualifying disabilities under IDEA, the combination of which cause additional educational needs than either disability would alone?

a. Intellectual disabilities and blindness
b. Deafness and blindness
c. Intellectual disabilities and deafness
d. Autism and deafness

23. In the scenario in Question 65, which part is the antecedent?

a. The child screaming and running away
b. Placing the child in the large class
c. The child being socially shy
d. The teacher's concern regarding the child's shyness

Copyright © Mometrix Media. You have been licensed one copy of this document for personal use only. Any other reproduction or redistribution is strictly prohibited. All rights reserved.
This content is provided for test preparation purposes only and does not imply an endorsement by Mometrix of any particular political, scientific, or religious point of view.

24. Informed consent is required for all of the following instances except:

a. Provide services
b. Evaluate the student
c. Re-evaluate the student
d. Providing routine instruction

25. A manifestation determination review (MDR) must be conducted within how many days of a decision to change a SPED student's placement due to disciplinary reasons?

a. 5
b. 10
c. 15
d. 30

26. In the first week of school, a resource teacher asks her high school students to make lists of things they know how to do well. How is this activity most useful to the teacher?

a. It establishes a feeling of success in her students from the start
b. It is an informal assessment of their writing skills and gives the teacher an idea of each student's interests and abilities
c. It is a formal assessment of prior knowledge
d. It invites further discussion of each student's unique contributions and will help the class bond with mutual respect

27. A re-evaluation must be conducted after the initial evaluation:

a. Every year
b. Every three years
c. When it appears the child is no longer making progress under the current IEP
d. Every six months

28. What are some benefits or drawbacks of measurement by permanent product?

a. The practitioner is free to do other tasks while the behavior is occurring.
b. The practitioner may make more mistakes than when using direct observation, since he/she is not directly observing the behavior as it occurs.
c. The practitioner may miss some behaviors which occur at times that are inaccessible to the researcher.
d. Multiple observers are needed to make the assessment.

29. Jose, a Hispanic student in 5th grade English, speaks fluent English and has lived in the United States his entire life. He does, however, have some differing cultural values, such as being uncomfortable with competitions, from mainstream America. His teacher planned a spelling bee, but quickly realized that for Jose, this would be awkward and an uncomfortable way for him to learn. A culturally-sensitive, alternative approach to help Jose learn spelling would be:

a. Placing him in a collaborative learning group with other students to work on spelling words
b. Calling out spelling words and having the students spell them on small white boards. Students then hold up the boards so the teacher can see them while she keeps tally marks on the board for each student
c. Playing a game of hangman
d. Continue with the spelling bee and invite Jose's family, using it as a cultural teaching opportunity

Copyright © Mometrix Media. You have been licensed one copy of this document for personal use only. Any other reproduction or redistribution is strictly prohibited. All rights reserved.
This content is provided for test preparation purposes only and does not imply an endorsement by Mometrix of any particular political, scientific, or religious point of view.

30. An ARD meeting has been scheduled for Glenda, a student with LEP. Among the ARD committee members, there must be one who:

a. Can interpret to and from Glenda's native language to ensure that she can understand said the meeting's discussion
b. Is a Language Proficiency Assessment Committee (LPAC) representative
c. Will take the final printed ARD paperwork and make sure it is translated into the child's native language
d. The child's ESL teacher

31. IDEA includes two fundamental requirements:

a. The child must receive specialized services which are offered to the parents, even if some of it may have to be paid for by the parents, and the parents must give consent to all services to be received.
b. The child must, to the extent appropriate, receive a free and appropriate public education and be placed in the least restrictive environment that would best serve the child.
c. The child must be placed in the least restrictive environment that would best serve his/her, and receive a free and appropriate education, except when some services must be paid for by the parents.
d. The child must be immediately evaluated if referred to special education, and all services deemed appropriate should be offered to the child and his/her parents.

32. Measurement by permanent product does not:

a. Take place after the behavior has occurred
b. Measure the lasting effect of the behavior on the environment
c. Analyze products left behind by the behavior
d. Quantify the cause of the behavior

33. After a parent or guardian requests to see a special education student's folder, how long does the school have to provide it?

a. 30 days
b. 45 days
c. 60 days
d. 90 days

Refer to the following for question 34:

Christina is an 11th-grade student who receives special education services due to an emotional disturbance and has a hard time completing any work due to frustration. When Christina becomes frustrated enough, she tends to lash out verbally to nearby people.

34. Which of the following strategies would be most appropriate for creating a supportive learning environment for Christina?

a. Ensuring that everyone in the class speaks their opinion
b. Pairing students together to share their experiences
c. Asking probing questions to open up the discussion
d. Collaborating with the students to set group parameters

Copyright © Mometrix Media. You have been licensed one copy of this document for personal use only. Any other reproduction or redistribution is strictly prohibited. All rights reserved.
This content is provided for test preparation purposes only and does not imply an endorsement by Mometrix of any particular political, scientific, or religious point of view.

35. Which of the following does not demonstrate cultural competency from service providers?

a. Communicating openly with the student's family, using a translator, if needed
b. Assessing and evaluating the student's needs based on the minority group to which they belong
c. Determining placement and instructional decisions based on the student's needs
d. Teachers employing culturally appropriate instructional materials

36. In the IEP process, which of the following takes place first?

a. Referral
b. Eligibility
c. Identification
d. Development

37. Assessing a student's performance by having him/her create a portfolio of his/her work in a class exemplifies which type of assessment?

a. Observation
b. Formal assessment
c. Authentic assessment
d. Interviewing

38. If the ARD committee determines that a child must take an alternate assessment on a particular state or district-wide assessment, all of the following must be true except:

a. A statement must be provided in the child's IEP explaining why the selected assessment is appropriate for the child
b. A statement must be provided in the child's IEP regarding why the child cannot participate in the regular assessment
c. Monitor the short-term and annual goals of the original assessment
d. Annual goals must be included to assist in monitoring the student's progress towards meeting the state standards tested in the specified test

39. In the scenario in Question 65, which part is the consequence?

a. The child screaming and running away
b. The child being able to avoid any social interaction by leaving
c. The child getting into trouble for running out of class
d. The child not learning how to be more socially expressive

40. Educational diagnosticians working with early childhood-aged children should be aware of which of the following:

a. Early childhood-aged children still have to meet the same eligibility requirements as all other students in order to receive special education services under IDEA.
b. These children are rarely eligible for special education services under IDEA, since it is so hard to diagnose children in this age range.
c. Children ages 3-5 can qualify for special education services under IDEA if it can be shown that they have developmental delays which make them eligible to receive services.
d. These children are not permitted to be served under IDEA. They may only receive services under Section 504.

Copyright © Mometrix Media. You have been licensed one copy of this document for personal use only. Any other reproduction or redistribution is strictly prohibited. All rights reserved.
This content is provided for test preparation purposes only and does not imply an endorsement by Mometrix of any particular political, scientific, or religious point of view.

41. As part of the Texas Administrative Code, Educational Diagnosticians are required to do all of the following except:

a. Develop collaborative relationships with families, educators, the school, and related service personnel, and disregard FERPA in these collaborations
b. Understand and apply knowledge of ethical and professional practices, roles, and responsibilities
c. Know and demonstrate skills necessary for scheduling, time management, and organization
d. Understand and apply knowledge of ethnic, linguistic, cultural, and socioeconomic diversity and the significance of student diversity for evaluation, planning, and instruction.

42. All of the following factors should be ruled out as causes of low achievement before making a disability diagnosis of a Learning Disorder except:

a. Poverty, limited English proficiency, and cultural factors
b. Poor attendance
c. Emotional disorder or intellectual disabilities
d. Early developmental issues

43. In order to conduct an FBA, a diagnostician must first formulate hypotheses about the purpose of a problem behavior. What must the diagnostician do next while conducting the FBA?

a. Use functional analysis to test the hypothesis
b. Develop interventions based on the function of the behavior
c. Gather information
d. Recruit a team of specialists to conduct the FBA

44. Which of the following statements is NOT true regarding the enrollment of students from minority groups (such as African-American, Hispanic, or Asian-American) in special education?

a. Asian-Americans are typically over-represented in special education
b. Hispanics are typically over-represented in special education
c. African-Americans are typically over-represented in special education
d. Native Americans are typically over-represented in special education

45. Which of the following would be the best preventive measure when working with a student that struggles with following directions?

a. Modeling how a student follows directions
b. Teaching the rules at the beginning of class
c. Giving the student consequence choices
d. Meeting with the student to discuss the behavior

46. The mean score on the Stanford-Binet V and the Wechsler IQ tests is:

a. 10
b. 50
c. 100
d. 115

Copyright © Mometrix Media. You have been licensed one copy of this document for personal use only. Any other reproduction or redistribution is strictly prohibited. All rights reserved.
This content is provided for test preparation purposes only and does not imply an endorsement by Mometrix of any particular political, scientific, or religious point of view.

47. According to the Procedural Safeguards, what is the correct order of services given to a student who has been referred to special education?

a. Informed consent, evaluation, services, re-evaluation
b. Evaluation, informed consent, services, re-evaluation
c. Prior written notice, evaluation, services, re-evaluation
d. Prior written notice, informed consent, evaluation, services

48. A socially withdrawn child has an FBA conducted and a BIP written. The BIP specifies that this child will be placed in a large class in order to draw him/her out socially. The child reacts by screaming and running away, instead of interacting with peers. What is wrong with this BIP?

a. It uses positive reinforcement, but the wrong outcome was pursued.
b. It used negative reinforcement, but it should have been more thorough and considered this outcome.
c. It used negative reinforcement, but the wrong specified behavior was pursued.
d. The BIP needs more time to be effective

49. Ways to help to overcome disabilities in diverse populations include all of the following except:

a. Providing these students with a high-quality education
b. Making education relevant to them
c. Anchoring instruction to their culture and background
d. Instruction that fosters competition

50. When evaluating a student with a medical diagnosis of attention-deficit/hyperactivity disorder, what should the educational diagnostician know about how this disorder?

a. Children with attention-deficit/ hyperactivity disorder show significant variability in how much their educational performance is adversely affected by the disorder.
b. Children who have a medical diagnosis of attention-deficit / hyperactivity disorder automatically qualify for special education services under IDEA.
c. Children who have attention-deficit/hyperactivity disorder which significantly affects their educational performance are eligible to receive special education services under the IDEA disability category of ADHD.
d. The diagnosis of attention-deficit/hyperactivity disorder can be made by either a medical doctor or by the educational diagnostician.

51. A psychometric test serves as all of the following except:

a. A sample of behavior
b. A predictor of future behavior
c. A stand-alone evaluation
d. A multi-method approach

Copyright © Mometrix Media. You have been licensed one copy of this document for personal use only. Any other reproduction or redistribution is strictly prohibited. All rights reserved.
This content is provided for test preparation purposes only and does not imply an endorsement by Mometrix of any particular political, scientific, or religious point of view.

52. A student has diagnoses of both Asperger's Syndrome and emotional disturbance. The student's ARD committee found that the child's educational performance was substantially affected by his emotional disturbance, but not as a result of his symptoms related to Asperger's syndrome. Which of the following would be the most appropriate IDEA disability category for this student?

a. Emotional Disturbance
b. Asperger's Syndrome
c. Autism and Emotional Disturbance
d. Other Health Impairment and Emotional Disturbance

53. An average IQ score falls within average range when you add (plus or minus the standard error of measurement):

a. One standard deviation below and above to the mean score
b. One standard error of measurement above and below to the mean score
c. Two standard deviations below and above to the mean score
d. Two standard errors of measurement above and below to the mean score

54. Since some culturally diverse students may possess schemata which do not match those of the culture for which various school texts were written, how can teachers help these students counteract this discrepancy in the classroom?

a. Allow students to find out through study and testing what they are supposed to understand about the texts.
b. Discuss with the students' parents the students' inability to follow along with the required curriculum in the class.
c. Refer the students to special education for an evaluation.
d. Provide methods, such as graphic organizers and reading chapter previews, for these students to build background knowledge to connect the text's schemata with their own.

55. Another method of measuring behavior is time sampling. Which explanation best defines time sampling?

a. Recording whether a targeted behavior occurs throughout an entire time interval
b. Recording whether a targeted behavior occurs at the very end of a time interval
c. Recording whether a targeted behavior occurs at randomized times throughout the interval
d. Observing and recording behavior during intervals or at specific moments of time

56. Which of the following is not an example of a modification to a student's curriculum?

a. Having the student read texts on his/her grade level according to his/her FIE, even if it is lower than the grade level in which the student is placed
b. Changing the student's IEP goals to match the level at which he/she tested in his/her evaluation, even if it does not match TEKS for the student's grade level
c. Allowing the student to receive a copy of class notes, which are not given to other students, from the teacher
d. Having the student focus on learning math concepts which, according to his/her FIE, are at the student's grade level in math, even if it is lower than the grade level in which the student is placed.

Copyright © Mometrix Media. You have been licensed one copy of this document for personal use only. Any other reproduction or redistribution is strictly prohibited. All rights reserved.
This content is provided for test preparation purposes only and does not imply an endorsement by Mometrix of any particular political, scientific, or religious point of view.

57. Joseph has Down syndrome. He can communicate with short, simple verbal phrases. He can read only a few words that he learned over a long time. He lives just a few blocks from his school. His area is not served by the school bus system. His teacher has a goal for Joseph to learn the directions to and from school so his mother will no longer need to accompany him. Which of these would be a good way for the teacher to work with him on this goal?

a. Send Joseph out first with a map, monitoring him remotely.
b. Send Joseph out first with written directions and shadow him from a distance.
c. Walk with Joseph, prompting him to verbalize the route until he learns it.
d. Gradually decrease the number of days his mother walks with him

58. Annual goals which are included in each child's special education IEP must be:

a. Given to the parents every six weeks
b. Given to the parents every six weeks with progress noted
c. Described in terms that can be formally measured
d. Described in terms which are left to each subject teacher's subjective discretion to decide if the objectives have or have not been met

59. You are a parent attending the ARD of your child, Jason. The ARD committee creates an Individualized Education Plan (IEP) which the group views as the most appropriate and helpful for Jason. However, you, as the parent, disagree with some aspects of it. After discussing your differing viewpoints, you still cannot come to an agreement with the rest of the ARD committee. You decide to check and sign "Disagree" on the ARD Committee record sheet. The school then has the right to:

a. Implement their suggested IEP anyway, as long as the school gave you prior written notice that this would be their right and you have consented to the initial provision of services
b. Do nothing without your consent at any point in the special education process
c. Do nothing without a unanimous vote of "Agree" on the record of the ARD meeting and the IEP that was recommended
d. Change the IEP to fit what the parent suggests since providing those services would be better than providing no services.

60. Transition services, which begin being provided at age 16, do not include:

a. Higher education and training
b. Employment
c. Independent Living
d. Medical care

61. What is the most important or useful part of the functional behavior assessment?

a. Learning if the student is aware of his/her behavior
b. Recognizing what behaviors the student is engaging in
c. Seeing if various observer ratings of the student's behavior match with each other
d. Discerning the purpose or motivation behind the problem behavior

Copyright © Mometrix Media. You have been licensed one copy of this document for personal use only. Any other reproduction or redistribution is strictly prohibited. All rights reserved.
This content is provided for test preparation purposes only and does not imply an endorsement by Mometrix of any particular political, scientific, or religious point of view.

62. To receive special education services under the disability category of Emotional Disturbance, all but which one of the following characteristics could make a child eligible under IDEA?

a. An inability to learn which cannot be explained by intellectual, sensory, or health factors
b. A diagnosis of schizophrenia
c. A general pervasive mood of unhappiness or depression
d. Social maladjustment

63. Jessica is a six-year-old kindergarten student. Which description may indicate typical language development?

a. She speaks in sentences of five to six words.
b. She has a vocabulary of 500 words.
c. She holds up her fingers to tell her age.
d. She uses phrases such as "me want"

64. In order to maintain compliance with ethical guidelines for educational diagnosticians, if a diagnostician is assigned a student to assess or evaluate a student who he/she knows from outside the school setting, the diagnostician should:

a. Use the additional information from personal knowledge in the assessment
b. Realize that previously formed opinions of the student may cause the diagnostician to be biased and, therefore, decline to be the diagnostician assigned to evaluate that particular student
c. Assess the student, but have an additional diagnostician review the assessment to make sure that no bias entered the assessment
d. Leave the diagnostician selection up to the student

65. One method of measuring behavior is event recording. What is this?

a. Recording the motivation behind a behavior which occurs
b. Recording with another observer both of your views regarding the motivation of a behavior and comparing both notes for consistency
c. Detecting and recording the number of times a behavior occurs
d. Timing how long a specific behavior lasts

66. On the Stanford-Binet V and the Wechsler IQ tests, which range of scores would fall within one standard deviation below and above the mean?

a. 40- 60
b. 80-120
c. 85 -115
d. 30- 70

Copyright © Mometrix Media. You have been licensed one copy of this document for personal use only. Any other reproduction or redistribution is strictly prohibited. All rights reserved.
This content is provided for test preparation purposes only and does not imply an endorsement by Mometrix of any particular political, scientific, or religious point of view.

67. Adhering to the Texas Administrative Code section which states that diagnosticians should develop collaborative relationships with families, educators, the school, the community, outside agencies, and related service personnel, what should a diagnostician encourage of parents of a student in special education with a reading disability to do?

a. Learn some reading intervention strategies used at school and to use them also at home as much as possible
b. Communicate with the parents as much as possible about how the school, not the parents, will help the child learn the necessary skills for compensating for his/her reading disability
c. Ensure the parents are invited to the annual ARD meeting where progress can be discussed
d. Push for large amounts of practice reading at home, especially in front of others

68. After a student's IEP is written, by law the school must

a. Provide a copy to the parents at no cost
b. Provide a copy which the parents must pay for
c. Provide a copy only if the parents request one
d. Not provide a copy as this is a legal document

69. Response to Intervention (RTI) is:

a. Parents, classroom teacher, special education teacher and other caring persons stage an intervention to express how a student's socially unacceptable behavior upsets them
b. An opportunity for a student to openly and freely respond to specific interventions without fear of reprimand
c. A strategy for diagnosing learning disabilities in which a student receives research-supported interventions to correct an academic delay. If the interventions do not result in considerable improvement, the failure to respond suggests causal learning disabilities
d. A formal complaint lodged by a parent or guardian in response to what they consider an intrusion by a teacher into private matters

70. The underrepresentation of Asian-Americans in special education may be the result of all of the following except:

a. Parental and student reluctance to acknowledge the presence of a disability, which in some Asian cultural groups may be considered shameful
b. Teacher bias towards Asian-American students as being better students than students from other cultures, resulting in lower than needed referrals to special education
c. Inappropriate evaluation conducted by the diagnostician with regard to cultural issues
d. Genetic predisposition for fewer disabilities in many Asian populations

71. When evaluating a student who displays deficits on norm-referenced achievement test(s) and has an IQ in the average range, the educational diagnostician must keep all of the following in mind about how a student may meet the criteria for having a Learning Disability under IDEA except:

a. This discrepancy alone is not enough to show that a student has a Learning Disability.
b. Additional factors such as criterion-referenced tests, curriculum-based tests, work samples, response to intervention, parent and teacher input, and attendance need to be evaluated and all of the results should be analyzed.
c. Early developmental issues can be disregarded if the discrepancy is being evaluated in late elementary school or later.
d. To qualify as having a learning disability, it must be determined that the student fails to achieve adequately when provided appropriate instruction by highly qualified teachers.

Copyright © Mometrix Media. You have been licensed one copy of this document for personal use only. Any other reproduction or redistribution is strictly prohibited. All rights reserved.
This content is provided for test preparation purposes only and does not imply an endorsement by Mometrix of any particular political, scientific, or religious point of view.

72. A child is referred to special education for experiencing significant difficulty with his or her educational performance in math and English. When conducting an assessment and evaluation of the student, what should the diagnostician keep in mind about the requirements of finding a student eligible for special education services under IDEA?

a. Achievement and intelligence tests which are given to the student will clearly indicate in which disability category, if any, the child will be eligible for under IDEA.
b. The educational diagnostician has the final word regarding the disability category in which the student is eligible for special education services under IDEA.
c. Information from a variety of sources- such as parent interviews, teacher interviews, investigation into medical history, and understanding of cultural background- has to be included in the assessment before proper eligibility can be determined.
d. There are no other legal support and service options available to the student if he/she does not qualify for any of the IDEA disability categories.

73. Ms. Hutchinson is supervising her small class at lunch. Ann, who has Down syndrome, displays some rude behaviors at times. On this day, she deliberately breaks wind at the table, which offends and "grosses out" the others, who complain about it. Ann does not seem concerned and does not apologize. Later, the other students are still upset with her, and Ann does not understand why. In a 1:1 conversation with Ann, Ms. Hutchinson asks her, "What if one of the other students passed gas at the table while you were eating?" Ann looks surprised and then disgusted as she imagines this. "Oh!" she responds, "that would be awful!" "Yes," Ms. Hutchinson agrees, "so now do you see why they were upset when you did it?" "Yes," says Ann, and she apologizes to the others, promising not to do this again. What is the best description of what Ms. Hutchinson did here?

a. She enforced more proper manners by inducing guilt in Ann for her inappropriate behavior.
b. She modeled some more appropriate behavior for Ann by demonstrating a better example.
c. She aided self-awareness, self-control, and self-management by enabling perspective-taking.
d. She increased self-reliance and self-confidence in Ann by treating her as a respected equal.

74. Curriculum-based assessment:

a. Is a formal assessment
b. Does not use standardized measurement procedures
c. Tests items in a student's required curriculum
d. Is not useful for peer-comparison

75. Juan, a Mexican student in the 11th grade, moved to the United States three years ago. He speaks English fairly well but is not quite fluent. He is in special education. What kinds of instructional planning ideas should the diagnostician keep in mind when writing suggested interventions in the FIE and providing feedback to Juan's ESL teachers?

a. Use English at Juan's fluency level and introduce complex ideas in the student's native language.
b. Use English all the time and only explain what is said in Juan's native language if he asks or seems confused.
c. Teach all material initially in Juan's native language to ensure proper understanding, and once understanding is confirmed go over it again in English.
d. Teach all material initially in Juan's native language and only use English when testing over the material.

Copyright © Mometrix Media. You have been licensed one copy of this document for personal use only. Any other reproduction or redistribution is strictly prohibited. All rights reserved.
This content is provided for test preparation purposes only and does not imply an endorsement by Mometrix of any particular political, scientific, or religious point of view.

76. How long should a student's current IEP, referral sheet, and initial consent form be kept on file?

a. While the documents are current, then they may be discarded
b. For the duration of the current school year, then they may be discarded
c. They should be kept on file regardless of how long the student has been in special education
d. Until the student moves to another campus or school disctrict

77. Which of the following best describes the goal of implementing a functional curriculum for students with disabilities?

a. To teach independent living skills to students
b. To teach communication skills to students
c. To teach basic subjects to students
d. To teach everyday tasks to students

78. Any student work, files, or records which need to be disposed of should be:

a. Put into the recycler
b. Thrown in the trash can
c. They should never be thrown away.
d. Shredded

79. Which of the following is not a concern the diagnostician needs to keep in mind when working with culturally and linguistically diverse (CLD) students?

a. They may be denied access to the general education curriculum.
b. They may be placed into separate programs with a limited curriculum.
c. They may get to receive extra beneficial academic and social services even if they are misclassified in a disability category.
d. They may be stigmatized by a misclassification.

80. For a student with vision loss, what might be an appropriate accommodation for him/her?

a. Not having to do any of the required reading
b. Exempt the student from any classes which require reading
c. Have their teachers give the student his/her work in a larger font
d. Give the student reading assignments in Braille

81. The renewal date of a Standard Certificate for an Educational Diagnostician will be how many years after the last day of the certificate holder's birth month?

a. 3
b. 4
c. 5
d. 6

82. One standard deviation above the mean encompasses what percentage of the normed sample?

a. 15%
b. 50%
c. 34%
d. 63%

Copyright © Mometrix Media. You have been licensed one copy of this document for personal use only. Any other reproduction or redistribution is strictly prohibited. All rights reserved.
This content is provided for test preparation purposes only and does not imply an endorsement by Mometrix of any particular political, scientific, or religious point of view.

83. An accommodation includes all of the following except:

a. A change to what or how much is being taught in the TEKS content
b. A change in how the TEKS content will be taught, made accessible, or assessed
c. Can be used school-wide to address the needs of all students
d. A tool which provides equal access and understanding of the material to the student

84. In meetings, diagnosticians regularly present as percentile ranks rather than standard scores. The benefit(s) of doing this is/ are:

a. To adhere to the disciplinary rule that a Registered Professional Educational Diagnostician shall communicate test results in such a manner as to guard against misinterpretation or misuse
b. To provide a broader scope of information about the student than just his/her standard score
c. To keep the ARD committee from making false comparisons among students
d. That percentile ranks, while more difficult for parents to understand than standard scores, are better understood by educators and other ARD committee members

85. Which of the following is the most useful skill for a learning objective in a general education setting for seventh-grade students with specific learning disabilities in the area of writing?

a. Writing sentences
b. Writing paragraphs
c. Writing essays
d. Writing words

86. Sam has an orthopedic impairment which makes administering many standardized assessments difficult since he cannot fully use his hands and arms to manipulate objects. A diagnostician should adhere to the following guidelines when selecting a test:

a. Select a test which does not need to be modified or one which requires the least amount of modification from its original version to be fairly administered.
b. The diagnostician cannot administer any tests in this situation since all standardized assessments require manipulation of at least some objects.
c. Administer all the sections of the test that do not require manipulation of objects and use the sub-scores obtained to make placement decisions.
d. Appropriately modify any test from its original version to be fairly administered in order to asses Sam.

87. A child has a traumatic brain injury which was acquired during birth trauma. How would the student would qualify for special education services?

a. An autism spectrum diagnosis
b. An emotional disturbance diagnosis
c. A traumatic brain injury diagnosis
d. A diagnosis of intellectual disabilities, deafness, or blindness resulting from the traumatic brain injury

Copyright © Mometrix Media. You have been licensed one copy of this document for personal use only. Any other reproduction or redistribution is strictly prohibited. All rights reserved.
This content is provided for test preparation purposes only and does not imply an endorsement by Mometrix of any particular political, scientific, or religious point of view.

88. What kind of service is providing a hearing aid for a child in special education with some hearing loss?

a. An accommodation
b. A modification
c. Assistive technology
d. The school does not have to provide hearing aids to students with hearing loss.

89. Susan is a third-grade student with autism undergoing a special education evaluation for concerns with her behavior. How can the results of behavior rating scales assist in understanding the instruction that Susan may benefit from?

a. Asking teachers to fill out forms
b. Asking teachers to observe Susan in different settings
c. Asking teachers to interview Susan
d. Asking teachers to give Susan a written assessment

90. "OI" stands for the IDEA disability category of:

a. Other Health Impairment
b. Osteopathic Impairment
c. Orthopedic Impairment
d. Orthodontic Impediment

Copyright © Mometrix Media. You have been licensed one copy of this document for personal use only. Any other reproduction or redistribution is strictly prohibited. All rights reserved.
This content is provided for test preparation purposes only and does not imply an endorsement by Mometrix of any particular political, scientific, or religious point of view.

Answer Key and Explanations

1. A: Answer A. defines a norm-referenced test. Examples of norm referenced tests are the SAT, ACT, GRE, the Stanford-Binet V, the WAIS, the WISC-IV, and the WPPSI-III. Answer B. defines a criterion-referenced test. State assessments, including the STAAR Tests, where a certain score is necessary in order to pass, exemplifies a criterion-referenced test.

2. D: Providing students with many opportunities to read encourages reading proficiency by allowing them more reading practice. Providing the students with choices of reading materials (A) has also been shown to enhance their motivation to read because they have more control and choice than they do when reading only teacher-chosen materials, and because they can choose to read something that is personally appealing to them. When teachers can show students what is meaningful in what they read, students are more interested in reading (B). Teachers can also enhance students' motivation to read by making the activity fun (C).

3. A: While FERPA is more concerned with confidentiality than IDEA is, IDEA does specifically address confidentiality. The Education for All Handicapped Children Act of 1975 eventually evolved into the current IDEA law. HIPAA, while concerned about confidentiality, concerns patient files in a healthcare setting.

4. A: The State Board for Educator Certification. Although it falls under TEA, TEA does not grant the certifications; the State Board does. There is a Texas Educational Diagnostician's Association, but they do not issue certificates. Colleges and universities are not allowed to offer certifications either.

5. B: A modification is a change to what is being taught and, thus, changes the TEKS content. This can be either a change in what the student is expected to learn or a reduction in the number of concepts to be learned. This is not simply a change in approach to instruction, attempting to help the child learn by offering the material in a variety of formats, or offering supports such as graphic organizers, class notes, or peer tutoring.

6. A: But this should not replace the teaching of basic computation skills as outlined in the TEKS. Using a calculator would be an appropriate accommodation if the student has the ability to reason or is still being taught how to reason mathematically, but has a disability which affects mathematics calculation. The use of a calculator can help avoid the stress associated with speed and accuracy pressures, and can also simplify otherwise unwieldy and multi-step calculations.

7. D: A school which implements an RtI system still has an obligation to identify students with disabilities. Parents, teachers or anyone else can request a referral at any time regardless of whether the child is receiving interventions through an RtI system or not. A child does not need to advance through the multi-tiers of the RtI system before a referral is made. In certain circumstances, a student may have progressed through multiple tiers without achieving academic success. In this situation, a disability should be suspected and a referral must be made. While processing the referral and determining whether or not the child should be evaluated for special education services within required timelines, a school may continue RtI interventions which have already been initiated.

8. B: According to the federal guidelines, the baseline age at which a student must be invited to ARD committee meetings is 16, though this guideline may be further augmented by state requirements. A child must be invited to the ARD committee meeting when transition services will be discussed. Transition services are a coordinated set of activities designed to help the child move from school

Copyright © Mometrix Media. You have been licensed one copy of this document for personal use only. Any other reproduction or redistribution is strictly prohibited. All rights reserved.
This content is provided for test preparation purposes only and does not imply an endorsement by Mometrix of any particular political, scientific, or religious point of view.

to post-school activities. Those activities begin by age 16 with an examination of transition issues including the appropriate courses of study based on transition goals. The IEP must include transition services needed to assist the child in reaching those goals.

9. C: Information on specific tests and their appropriateness for certain subgroups is frequently detailed in the test's manual or in testing resources, such as the Mental Measurements Yearbook. Additionally, the sample of students which was used to develop the test can be examined to see if it included students from the student's subgroup. If it did not, there is little likelihood that the test can be appropriate for that subgroup since they were not included in the standardization of the test. All students should not be given the same assessments, regardless of diversity issues. If the test is not valid and reliable for a certain subgroup, it should not be used for that subgroup. This applies not only to diversity issues but to other subgroups, such as specific disorders, as well. Diagnosticians need to make sure that each test is valid and reliable for the particular student to whom they are administering it, or find an alternate test which is valid for the student's subgroup.

10. C: When standardizing tests, it is important to administer the test to a representative sample of test takers under clearly specified conditions. The test formulators must score and interpret the data to use as a context for future test takers of the same test.

11. A: Typing and dictating are accommodations, but a handwriting disability would not require any modifications to be added to Klara's IEP. Her disability can be addressed through various accommodations, which do not change the curriculum or course material to be mastered, but simply allow Klara to have her answers either recorded by a scribe or typed by herself, depending on the situation and her preferences.

12. B: The services provided should ensure that the child is advancing appropriately toward his/her designated goals and educated with and participates with nondisabled children as much as is appropriate for that child. B is incorrect because of LRE.

13. C: Autism. The "disability category" qualifying a child for special education and related services differs from the child's medical "diagnosis." Under IDEA, the child may be found eligible for services under 13 disability categories. Asperger's Syndrome falls in the category of Autism. There is no Asperger's Syndrome category under IDEA.

14. A: Since John is 18 years old and a legal adult, the legal requirement for consent for services which is mandatory under IDEA now falls to him, rather than his parents, even if the ARD committee and his parents disagree with John's decision. His parents can still be invited to any final ARD meetings that they will have and can voice their opinions, but the consent for services must now fall to John, and he has the right to reject them.

15. B: Error. A student's score on an assessment will always equal his/her true score plus any error which was introduced to the test. Sources of error may include: the way the test was constructed, whether or not the test was administered correctly and according to standardized procedures, and test scoring and interpretation. Additionally, other sources of error may involve people being dishonest on self-report measures, informants used to rate other individuals without displaying an objective view of that person, culturally-biased tests, having a poor norming sample, inappropriate sample size, confirmatory bias, drawing inferences of causation, and availability bias among others.

16. B: 200 clock hours must be completed in continuing education within each 5- year licensure period. Diagnosticians are responsible for obtaining and keeping records of continuing education coursework.

Copyright © Mometrix Media. You have been licensed one copy of this document for personal use only. Any other reproduction or redistribution is strictly prohibited. All rights reserved.
This content is provided for test preparation purposes only and does not imply an endorsement by Mometrix of any particular political, scientific, or religious point of view.

17. A: Answer B. has some merit since it can prevent parents from suing because they weren't given the Procedural Safeguards. It may also help parents more clearly understand the special education system and enable parents to more clearly describe their concerns. Since avoiding a lawsuit is not the goal of providing the Procedural Safeguards to parents, B. is not the best answer. C. is incorrect because the details are not reviewed in this publication, although the parents have the right to request to know which tests and evaluation methods have been or will be used for their child. Under some situations, D. may be true since parents who read and understand the Procedural Safeguards may have fewer questions, but this is not the intended result or the reason behind providing it. Another reason the document is provided is to make sure parents are aware of their rights.

18. C: All of the others professionals would be appropriate ARD committee members. The following is a list of appropriate ARD committee members:

- the parent
- at least one regular education teacher of the child
- at least one special education teacher or provider of the child
- a representative of the district
- a person who can interpret the instructional implications of the evaluation results
- if appropriate, the student
- other individuals who have knowledge or special expertise regarding the child and are invited by either the special education representative or the school, and if applicable:
- a certified teacher for the child with a suspected or documented Auditory Impairment
- (AI)
- a certified teacher for the child with a suspected or documented Visual Impairment (VI)
- an AI certified teacher and a VI certified teacher for the child with suspected or documented deaf-blindness
- a Career and Technology Education (CTE) representative for the child who is being considered for initial or continued placement
- a Language Proficiency Assessment Committee (LPAC) representative for a child who is who is LEP.

19. A: The TOWL is an evidence-based assessment of a student's basic writing skills because its results are norm-referenced and supported by experimental research results. The other choices are all equally effective methods of assessing basic student writing. However, "evidence-based" is less descriptive of these because they rely on individual teacher methods and/or individual student writing samples, but they are not proven by evidence from research studies and do not compare student results to those of normative student sample groups.

20. A: Additionally, ethical considerations must also be followed, and a practitioner may lose his/her licensure if the ethical considerations are not followed. It is possible to break both disciplinary rules and ethical guidelines; however, they are not the same. Disciplinary rules are governed by the Board of Registry and should be implemented consistently. It is possible for a person to break a disciplinary rule, pay his/her fine, and then be reinstated as a diagnostician.

21. A: This would only be true if the specific goal of the testing is to assess the student's functioning/achievement in an area related to English learning. Otherwise, the goal of the test is to assess the student and find out, depending on the nature of the test, various data such as IQ, achievement in a variety of subject areas, how things are going at home (in the case of an interview or questionnaire), and psychological issues. In order to get the most accurate information possible,

Copyright © Mometrix Media. You have been licensed one copy of this document for personal use only. Any other reproduction or redistribution is strictly prohibited. All rights reserved.
This content is provided for test preparation purposes only and does not imply an endorsement by Mometrix of any particular political, scientific, or religious point of view.

the student needs to be tested in a language in which he/she is fluent to make sure he/she understands the questions fully. B., C., and D., are all true.

22. B: There is a category of Deaf-Blindness; all of the other combinations would fall under the category of Multiple Disabilities. For all of these, they would only be used if the combination of the disabilities causes additional educational needs than either disability would alone.

23. B: Placing the child in the large class is the antecedent stimulus which prompts the behavior of her running out of the class and screaming. If the original problem behavior was being socially withdrawn, a FBA would have to be conducted to determine the antecedent stimulus for the withdrawn behavior. This can be determined through a variety of means, such as teacher reports, parent reports, self reports, observations, etc.

24. D: Informed consent must be given for each step of special education services. It must be in writing and in the parent's native language.

25. B: 10 days. When conducting the MDR, the team members must review all relevant information in the child's file, including the child's IEP, any teacher observations, and any relevant information provided by the child's parents. The members determine: (I) if the child's conduct was the direct result of the school's failure to implement the child's IEP; or (II) if the child's conduct was caused by or had a direct and substantial relationship to the child's disability. If the members determine that either clause is applicable, then the child's conduct must be considered a manifestation of his/her disability. If the child's conduct is a manifestation of his or her disability, the ARD committee must: conduct a functional behavioral assessment (FBA), unless the school had conducted a FBA before the behavior occurred that resulted in the change of placement, as well as implement a behavioral intervention plan (BIP) for the child. Where a BIP has already been developed, the ARD committee must review the BIP and modify it as necessary to address the behavior. If the child's conduct was the direct result of the school's failure to implement the child's IEP, the school must take immediate steps to remedy those deficiencies.

26. B: It is an informal assessment of their writing and also gives the teacher an idea of each student's interests, abilities and skills. This assignment gives the teacher an idea of her students' writing abilities at the beginning of the year. She can return to this piece of writing during the school year to assess progress.

27. B: Every three years. An exception to this law is if the parent and the school both agree that a re-evaluation is not necessary at that time. The re-evaluation begins with the school examining information from a variety of sources and determining if a full re-evaluation is needed. If the special education teacher decides that a re-evaluation is not needed, but the parent requests a full re-evaluation, a full re-evaluation must be provided.

28. A: Benefits of measurement by permanent product are: the practitioner is free to do other tasks while the behavior is taking place; it makes it possible to measure behaviors which occur at inconvenient or inaccessible times by measuring their effects, not the actual behavior; the measurement may be more complete, accurate, and continuous since the practitioner can take his/her time in measuring the effects of the behavior and/or can review his/her data multiple times for accuracy; and it can eliminate the need for multiple observers if the behavior's effects can be viewed multiple times.

29. A: Collaborative grouping will emphasize the qualities of working together as a team on a common task with a group of students, and will not involve competition. B. is better than a spelling

Copyright © Mometrix Media. You have been licensed one copy of this document for personal use only. Any other reproduction or redistribution is strictly prohibited. All rights reserved.
This content is provided for test preparation purposes only and does not imply an endorsement by Mometrix of any particular political, scientific, or religious point of view.

bee since Jose would not be in front of the class with everyone hearing his answers, but the approach still involves competition among students. C. This would still involve competition.

30. B: an LPAC representative for the child. An interpreter may also attend and can assist in interpreting for the parents. The child's ESL teacher may also attend, but for any child who is LEP, an LPAC representative must attend the ARD. The paperwork should also be given to the student's parents in their native language, but no person required to attend the ARD must do so.

31. B: A. and C. are incorrect because the parents should never have to pay for services which are deemed necessary and are recommended by the school. This is part of the free and appropriate public education (FAPE) mandate that is one of the two fundamental requirements of IDEA. The parents may choose to reject services offered or pay for services that are not recommended by the school.

32. D: Measurement by permanent product measures what a student has created or accomplished which can be measured after the fact, and that leaves a lasting effect on the environment. This method refers to measuring after the behavior occurred and measures the effect of the behavior, rather than the behavior itself.

33. B: 45 days

34. D: Although all of these strategies may be beneficial to certain students, those with emotional disturbances like Christina often are reluctant to share information. It would be valuable to hear their input on the expectations and parameters of the class in order to get an idea of what they might be comfortable with. They would be more likely to share their experiences if they helped establish the boundaries. Answer a is incorrect because ensuring that everyone speaks might not make all of the students in the class comfortable. Answer b is incorrect because pairing students in groups may not always be beneficial if the students are not comfortable with each other. Answer c is incorrect because asking probing questions might also be uncomfortable for students.

35. B: A student's needs should not be identified based on the minority group to which they belong, but diversity issues are kept in mind when making instructional plans so that these students receive the most individualized and culturally appropriate services available are all important for the diagnostician when working with not only these groups, but with all students. Service providers display cultural competency at the critical points in answer choices A., C., and D. Additionally, teachers who provide instruction prior to referral and the availability of culturally appropriate instructional materials must also display cultural competency.

36. A: After a student is referred to special education services by a teacher, parent, social services, or others, assessments are conducted to identify (C) the student as having a disability or not and, if so, to diagnose the specific disability and establish performance baselines for planning interventions and for comparison in evaluating progress. After identification, the IEP team uses assessment results to determine the student's eligibility (B) for special education and for which specific services. Then the team develops (D) the IEP.

37. C: Authentic assessment. Authentic assessments which focus on criterion-referenced comparisons, as well as process and products, yields both quantitative and qualitative feedback and involve a range of response models. Observations can involve ABC charting or charting the frequency of a specified behavior. A formal assessment would be a standardized test. Interviewing involves talking with parents, teachers, and the student to obtain information about how to teach the child.

Copyright © Mometrix Media. You have been licensed one copy of this document for personal use only. Any other reproduction or redistribution is strictly prohibited. All rights reserved.
This content is provided for test preparation purposes only and does not imply an endorsement by Mometrix of any particular political, scientific, or religious point of view.

38. C: The alternate test short-term goals will also be included as part of the annual goals when an alternate assessment is recommended. For any test, the school or district may decide to include short-term goals, as well as long-term goals as part of the annual goals for monitoring purposes.

39. B: The behavior of interest is how the child behaves socially (screaming and running away), which is the B in the ABC (antecedent-behavior-consequence) theory. The antecedent is placing the child in the large class. The consequence is avoiding having to engage in any social interaction which allows the child to avoid his/her feelings of anxiety about being in a large classroom.

40. C: In Texas, children ages 3-5 may receive special education services under IDEA for developmental delays. This category is called "Non-Categorical Early Childhood (NCEC)" in Texas. It includes delays in the child's physical, cognitive, communication, social, emotional, or adaptive development.

41. A: FERPA regulates collaborative relationships, and it must be followed in all circumstances.

42. D: Early developmental issues. Early developmental issues must be considered when making a disability diagnosis of a Learning Disorder.

43. A: Use functional analysis to test the hypothesis. In functional analysis, antecedents and consequences representing those in the person's natural environment are arranged so that separate effects on the problem behavior can be measured and observed. B. is the last step in an FBA, after the hypothesis has been tested and has evidence to support it. C. is the first step in an FBA.

44. A: Diagnosticians need to be aware that Asian-Americans are typically under-represented in special education; Hispanics are represented about as often as Caucasians; and African-Americans and Native Americans are typically over-represented in special education. The causes are complex and not easily explicated. Ensuring the students are accurately evaluated, the goal of eventually exiting special education is held foremost, and diversity issues are kept in mind when making instructional plans so that these students receive the most individualized and culturally appropriate services available are all important for the diagnostician when working with not only these groups, but with all students. Keep in mind that the goal is not to make all ethnicities have equal representation or to have an equal percentage of students in each disability category, but to assist qualifying students in the best way possible.

45. B: One of the most productive ways to prevent a student from misbehaving in class is to express what the expectations and ground rules for the class will be. Preventive strategies are designed to handle the misbehavior before it happens. Students who struggle with following directions will likely need to learn the rules of the class early on in order to try to limit this behavior. Answer a is incorrect because modeling how to follow directions likely would be ineffective as a preventive strategy if the behavior has already occurred. Answer c is incorrect because giving the student consequence choices would not be considered preventive because it has already happened. Answer d is incorrect because meeting with the student to discuss the behavior would also not be considered a preventive strategy and rather a reaction to the behavior.

46. C: 100. This means that students who score a 100 fall at the 50th percentile rank, meaning that 50% of the students that the test was normed against did worse or equal to the performance of that particular student.

47. D: The last step, not listed after services, is re-evaluation. A., B., and C. are all in the incorrect order.

Copyright © Mometrix Media. You have been licensed one copy of this document for personal use only. Any other reproduction or redistribution is strictly prohibited. All rights reserved.
This content is provided for test preparation purposes only and does not imply an endorsement by Mometrix of any particular political, scientific, or religious point of view.

48. B: Since negative reinforcement is meant to increase a specified behavior, in this case social interaction, it proves ineffective in this case. Also, this reaction would most likely have not occurred if a proper and thorough FBA had been conducted. Choosing not to do so would be unethical treatment of a problem behavior.

49. D: All of the approaches in answer choices A., B., and C. can help prevent and overcome disabilities in diverse populations. Diverse learners need to have instruction which helps them learn, fosters self-confidence, makes connections between their culture and that of mainstream America, and creates new experiences for them. Competition does not foster and inclusive learning environment.

50. A: If it cannot be shown that the disorder significantly and adversely affects the student's educational performance, it cannot be used to determine eligibility for special education services under IDEA. B. is incorrect because a medical diagnosis made by a doctor is not the same as a disability category under IDEA. Additionally, it has to be shown and agreed upon by an ARD committee that this disorder significantly and adversely affects the student's educational performance. According to IDEA, attention-deficit/hyperactivity disorder falls is called Other Health Impairment, or OHI. C. is incorrect because the disability category is OHI, not ADHD. D. is incorrect because the diagnosis of attention-deficit/hyperactivity disorder must be made by a doctor. After that, the IDEA disability category of OHI may be used when the student meets the additional criteria.

51. C: A test is only one part of the assessment process and does not stand alone in any evaluation of a student. Best practices in assessment dictate that the evaluator utilizes multiple methods: testing, interviews, observations, etc.; multiple informants: parents, student, teachers, etc.; and multiple settings: at school, at home, in the community, etc. Additionally, the test is only one sample of a student's behavior and must be combined with all of the above resources to form a more accurate picture of the student. This information can be used in making predictions of the student's future behavior.

52. A: Emotional Disturbance. Even if the child has a medical diagnosis of Asperger's Syndrome, under IDEA the child is only eligible for special education services for a disability category which significantly affects the student's educational performance. If the impairment is primarily due to an emotional disturbance rather than the Asperger's, then the category of Emotional Disturbance (ED) alone would be appropriate, as opposed to the IDEA category of Autism. Additionally, if both Asperger's and an emotional disturbance were found to be adversely affecting the student's educational performance, then both categories, Emotional Disturbance and Autism, would be appropriate disability categories.

53. A: One standard deviation below and above to the mean score. If the mean score of a certain norm-referenced test is 100, and if the student tests between 85 and 115 (plus or minus the standard error of measurement), the student is within the average range.

54. D: Culturally-sensitive instruction involves helping the students learn by honoring and working with the culture from which they hail. A. is incorrect because this simply leaves the student on his or her own to discern what he/she may not be able to understand. B. is incorrect because the problem is one of adequate instruction, not of parenting. C. is incorrect because nothing yet indicates that the student is not able to learn since appropriate teaching methods have not yet been employed. D. Other teaching strategies could be pre-teaching vocabulary in the text to the CLD students, showing a videotape related to the text to develop background knowledge of the subject, and engaging the students in a discussion about the topic.

Copyright © Mometrix Media. You have been licensed one copy of this document for personal use only. Any other reproduction or redistribution is strictly prohibited. All rights reserved.
This content is provided for test preparation purposes only and does not imply an endorsement by Mometrix of any particular political, scientific, or religious point of view.

55. D: A. refers to whole-interval recording, B. refers to momentary time sampling, and D. is correct.

56. C: All of the other answers are modifications. The FIE should show grade levels for various subjects and how the student is performing in them. If the student is performing below grade level, and he/she is in special education, then modifications should be provided which match the level and/or grade level of the student. The goal is to utilize proven interventions to help the student progress quickly and make as much progress as possible up to his/her current grade level. If a student is receiving modifications, he/she should also receive modifications on the TAKS test (TAKS-M).

57. C: Since Joseph has never walked the route alone, he would get lost if sent out on his own now. Therefore, option A is incorrect.

Sending Joseph out with written directions is not a good idea since he does not have good reading skills. He would likely get lost if he went out alone without prior practice in finding his way. A teacher shadowing him would have to catch up with him to redirect him when he went the wrong way or stopped when he did not know which way to go. Therefore, option B is incorrect.

Since Joseph is used to walking the route with his mother, it would be better to accompany him at first. Doing so would provide a point from which to transition gradually to walking alone. Unlike his mother, the teacher will be prompting him to verbalize the route. Since his expressive language skills are better than his reading skills, this is a more effective modality to help him learn the directions. Therefore, option C is correct.

Gradually decreasing the days his mother goes with him, such as by having her go four days and having him go alone one day, then having her go three days and having him go alone two days, is not a good idea. Joseph's mother has never taught him the route, so he does not know the directions and cannot find his way independently. Since he has always relied on his mother, he would get lost the first time he tried to go on his own. Therefore, option D is incorrect.

58. C: The goals and the progress towards the goals must be given to the parents, but the time frame is not specifically noted in the law. It may be every 3 weeks, 6 weeks, every semester, or some other interval of which the parent must be informed. The goals must be written in measurable terms so that progress can be objectively monitored, as in answer C., not subjectively monitored in the case of answer D.

59. A: The school must have given prior written notice that this is their right, however. Additionally, the school can only go forward if the parent has consented to the initial provision of services. Additionally, if the parent disagrees, they should be offered to have a recess not to exceed 10 days, after which the ARD committee will reconvene and attempt to come to a consensus again.

60. D: Higher education and training, employment, and independent living can all be part of a student's transition services, which are meant to help the student make the transition from high school to post-high school.

61. D: Without learning what is causing the problem or function of the behavior, it will be impossible to create an appropriate BIP to address the student's. For example, if a student misbehaves every time the teacher starts to teach spelling, and the result is that the teacher sends the student out of class for his misbehavior, a thorough FBA may find that the function of the misbehavior is actually to get out of the spelling portion of the class. In this case, the BIP will have to find an alternate way to deal with the student's behavior besides sending him out of class since

Copyright © Mometrix Media. You have been licensed one copy of this document for personal use only. Any other reproduction or redistribution is strictly prohibited. All rights reserved.
This content is provided for test preparation purposes only and does not imply an endorsement by Mometrix of any particular political, scientific, or religious point of view.

this consequence merely reinforces the problem behavior by giving the student exactly what he/she wants.

62. D: Social maladjustment, which is specifically listed in IDEA as not being included as a qualifying characteristic. It is important to note, however, that IDEA does include the following as a qualifying manifestation of Emotional Disturbance: An inability to build or maintain satisfactory interpersonal relationships with peers and teachers. Other characteristics which qualify as ED are inappropriate types of behavior or feelings under normal circumstances and a tendency to develop physical symptoms or fears associated with personal or school problems.

63. A: By the age of six, typical language development will include speaking in sentences of about five or six words. By this age, children tend to have a vocabulary of 2,000 or more words, so answer choice B is incorrect. Children at age six are also expected to communicate their age orally rather than with their fingers, so answer choice C is incorrect. They also no longer say simple phrases such as "me want," which eliminates answer choice D.

64. B: The diagnostician, who has any previously formed opinion of a student from outside of their professional role as a diagnostician, will be susceptible to bias in conducting the assessment. Therefore, he or she should not have any part in the assessment of that particular student.

65. C: Event recording simply records the number of times a behavior occurs or counts the number of occurrences and non-occurrence of a behavior. A. has more to do with conducting a functional behavioral analysis, and B. is similar, but also includes an element of inter-rater reliability. None of these are related to event recording. Neither is D., the length of time that a behavior lasts.

66. C: The mean on these two tests is 100, and one standard deviation is 15 points. The range of scores of one standard deviation below and one above would be 85 - 115. This is also the average range of scores on these tests.

67. A: B. is incorrect since it would inhibit communication and collaboration with the parents. The diagnostician or case manager should be doing C., but it does not fully address the need to encourage parents to try to work with the school's approach when the student is at home. D. is incorrect because excessive practice without helpful strategies will just frustrate the student.

68. A: Provide a copy to the parents at no cost to them. Additionally, the IEP must be provided in the parents' native language.

69. C: A strategy for diagnosing learning disabilities in which a student with an academic delay receives research-supported interventions to correct the delay. If the interventions do not result in considerable academic improvement, the failure to respond suggests causal learning disabilities.

70. D: Genetic predisposition for fewer disabilities in many Asian populations. Answer choices A., B., and C. may influence the underrepresentation of Asian-Americans in special education. Diagnosticians should be cautious though of forming stereotypes regarding any specific culture, whether they be positive or negative. A thorough evaluation which takes all factors into account needs to be conducted. Additionally, teachers should be trained in cultural issues and awareness.

71. C: Early developmental issues can be disregarded if the discrepancy is being evaluated in late elementary school or later. Early developmental issues should be considered, and answer choices A., B., and D. must all be kept in mind by the educational diagnostician when evaluating a student for a learning disorder.

Copyright © Mometrix Media. You have been licensed one copy of this document for personal use only. Any other reproduction or redistribution is strictly prohibited. All rights reserved.
This content is provided for test preparation purposes only and does not imply an endorsement by Mometrix of any particular political, scientific, or religious point of view.

72. C: A. is incorrect because while the tests given to the child are part of the eligibility process, they are only one part and other factors- such as background of the student, cultural considerations, the child's medical history, and teacher feedback- need to be taken into consideration. B. is incorrect because the ARD committee that will come to a conclusion based on all of the information presented at an ARD meeting. While the meeting's conclusion is not based on any one person's decision, important people such as the educational diagnostician, the parent(s), teachers of the student, and possibly the student, should attend the eligibility meeting. D. is incorrect because there are other options, such as Section 504 services, available to students who do not qualify for services under IDEA.

73. C: Ms. Hutchinson's technique was not accusatory or scolding. It would not likely induce guilt in someone as unrepentant as Ann. She asked a question that got Ann to consider others' points of view, so option A is incorrect.

Ms. Hutchinson did not model any behavior for Ann. She did not demonstrate anything to provide an example. She simply asked her two questions, so option B is incorrect.

By asking Ann how she would feel if another student had done to her what she did, Ms. Hutchinson helped her overcome her egocentric thinking. Due to her intellectual disabilities, Ann thinks on a concrete operational level, and it will frequently not occur to her on her own to consider another's perspective. She does have the ability to do this, though, with some help. Via this dialogue, Ms. Hutchinson got Ann to realize how the other students felt, so option C is correct.

Though Ms. Hutchinson did treat Ann with respect in this interaction and spoke to her as an equal, self-reliance and self-confidence were not issues that needed to be addressed in this case. Ann's rude behavior at the table did not show a lack of self-confidence. It definitely showed a lack of self-management, and it showed a lack of self-awareness in the sense of not appreciating the impact of her actions on others, so option D is incorrect.

74. C: Curriculum-based assessment is any assessment which tests items from the student's required curriculum. The assessment could take the form of a spelling probe, math test, reading tests with items on the student's grade level reading books, etc. While it is a type of informal assessment, rather than formal, the assessment does use a standardized procedure of measurement. Curriculum-based assessment can be useful for evaluators since the information gathered will tell how a student is doing compared to the educational requirements of that state, rather than the information gathered on achievement tests which are used nationwide and may or may not coordinate with a school's curriculum. Achievement assessments are still useful, however, in showing areas of weakness and can be used to compare to IQ scores when utilizing the discrepancy model as a way of identifying a learning-disabled student.

75. A: Teachers should be using English as much as possible, but only at levels where the student is fluent. Complex ideas should be introduced in the student's native language and then reviewed later in English. Additionally, the teacher may want to use visual aids to complement instruction and increase the student's comprehension. The teacher may also want to pre-teach vocabulary before beginning a new unit. B. is incorrect because speaking only English will not enable the student to learn complex concepts or ideas beyond his level of fluency. C. and D. are incorrect because English should be used as much as is possible according to the student's fluency level.

76. C: These are just some of the items which should be kept in a student's special education folder, regardless of how long he or she has been in special education. If the folder becomes too unwieldy and large, it can be split into multiple folders with the older IEPs, test protocols, and student work

Copyright © Mometrix Media. You have been licensed one copy of this document for personal use only. Any other reproduction or redistribution is strictly prohibited. All rights reserved.
This content is provided for test preparation purposes only and does not imply an endorsement by Mometrix of any particular political, scientific, or religious point of view.

kept in them. The current folder should still contain all of the answers listed, along with eligibility determination and any behavior plans.

77. A: Although all of these choices may be beneficial to students with disabilities, a functional curriculum is designed to teach students independent living skills. This curriculum typically replaces traditional secondary curriculum for certain students who may be candidates at the high school level. It tends to be designed for students who will struggle to live independently once they complete their schooling. Answer B is incorrect because although it may be helpful in developing communication skills, the sole purpose is not just for this communication development. Answer C is incorrect because the main goal of a functional curriculum is greater independence through functional life skills, which may also include communication and functional academics. Answer D is incorrect because the primary goal of functional curriculum is to teach independent living skills, not just to teach current everyday tasks.

78. D: Shredded. Some records need to be maintained for a period of years and should be stored after the student graduates. But other records, such as student's grades or schedule that are not needed long-term, should always be shredded.

79. C: A., B., and D. are all issues which the diagnostician should be aware of when working with CLD students. For C., being misclassified in a disability should not lead to services which are more beneficial, as the correct disability category and a thorough evaluation should lead to the most helpful instructional plan and interventions for a student.

80. C: A. and B. are not necessary if the vision loss can be corrected by any other means. Those would also be modifications -- very severe ones which would never be used, even for a blind student. Vision-impaired students could use braille or listen to their readings on tape. D. would not be necessary unless the student was blind and knew how to read braille.

81. C: 5 years after the last day of the person's birth month; Continuing education credits must also be completed.

82. C: 34. If you add one standard deviation below and above the mean on any norm-referenced test, regardless of its mean, this will encompass about 68% of the normed sample of the test on which it was standardized.

83. A: Accommodations do not change the "what" of the curriculum, but rather how the standard curriculum will be taught. All students are able to receive accommodations, but in a special education student's IEP sometimes certain accommodations are specifically explicated. Some examples of accommodations would be preferential seating, providing class notes to the student, books on tape, and extended time (unless the assignment is testing for speed).

84. A: B. is incorrect because it does not provide a broader scope of information. It just converts the score into a percentile rank, which actually will provide more information since the student can then be compared to his/her peers and their performances. C. is incorrect because standard scores do not allow for comparison among students, and D. is incorrect because it does not adhere to the disciplinary rule in answer A., which states that the test results must be communicated in a way that will be easiest to understand by all involved. Also, teachers and other members of the ARD will probably have little or no more understanding of the test scores than the student's parents.

85. B: Students in seventh grade with specific learning disabilities in the area of writing would be expected to be able to write a paragraph. Some students may have more skills than others, but most students would be able to write a paragraph. This objective may need to be modified for certain

Copyright © Mometrix Media. You have been licensed one copy of this document for personal use only. Any other reproduction or redistribution is strictly prohibited. All rights reserved.
This content is provided for test preparation purposes only and does not imply an endorsement by Mometrix of any particular political, scientific, or religious point of view.

students with more severe struggles, but a student with a specific learning disability that is appropriately placed would be expected to keep up with the curriculum. Answer a is incorrect because writing sentences would likely be a skill that students would have already mastered by this age. Answer C is incorrect because being able to write an essay likely would not be expected of seventh-grade students. Answer D is incorrect because simply writing words is a skill that these students already know.

86. A: The diagnostician should try to select a test with the least amount of modification necessary in order to preserve the reliability and validity of that test, especially if that test includes performance measures of intelligence or achievement. C. can be justified as long as the diagnostician acknowledges that the estimates of the scores on the other areas are truly rough estimates. Further, such rough estimates are never acceptable to use, in the absence of other data, when making placement decisions.

87. D: A diagnosis of intellectual disabilities, deafness, or blindness resulting from the traumatic brain injury. The disability category of Traumatic Brain Injury (TBI) in IDEA specifically lists TBI acquired during birth trauma as being excluded from that category. However, if this injury results in other problems for the child, such as intellectual disabilities, deafness or blindness, etc., then those categories may be used to qualify the child for special education services. In order to use Traumatic Brain Injury as a qualifying disability category, the injury must be caused by an external physical force (with the exception of birth trauma). Additionally, congenital or degenerative brain injuries do not fall under IDEA's TBI disability category.

88. C: Assistive technology. Providing a hearing aid is not an accommodation or a modification. The schools do have to pay for it, but are only required to provide the hearing aid while the child is at school.

89. A: Behavior rating scales are designed for teachers or parents to fill out in order to determine specific behaviors. These are typically compared with the results of other students in order to determine which behavior a student may struggle with. These can help to determine which accommodations or services need to be put in place in order to support students. Answer b is incorrect because simply performing evaluations would be helpful but would not be a part of the behavior rating scale. Answer c is incorrect because asking teachers to interview Susan would not indicate which behaviors are being exhibited in the classroom setting. Answer d is incorrect because a written assessment likely would not assist in evaluating student behavior.

90. C: Orthopedic Impairment refers to disorders of the skeletal and musculature systems. Other Health Impairment is "OHI," and there is no Osteopathic Impairment category in IDEA.

Copyright © Mometrix Media. You have been licensed one copy of this document for personal use only. Any other reproduction or redistribution is strictly prohibited. All rights reserved.
This content is provided for test preparation purposes only and does not imply an endorsement by Mometrix of any particular political, scientific, or religious point of view.

How to Overcome Test Anxiety

Just the thought of taking a test is enough to make most people a little nervous. A test is an important event that can have a long-term impact on your future, so it's important to take it seriously and it's natural to feel anxious about performing well. But just because anxiety is normal, that doesn't mean that it's helpful in test taking, or that you should simply accept it as part of your life. Anxiety can have a variety of effects. These effects can be mild, like making you feel slightly nervous, or severe, like blocking your ability to focus or remember even a simple detail.

If you experience test anxiety—whether severe or mild—it's important to know how to beat it. To discover this, first you need to understand what causes test anxiety.

Causes of Test Anxiety

While we often think of anxiety as an uncontrollable emotional state, it can actually be caused by simple, practical things. One of the most common causes of test anxiety is that a person does not feel adequately prepared for their test. This feeling can be the result of many different issues such as poor study habits or lack of organization, but the most common culprit is time management. Starting to study too late, failing to organize your study time to cover all of the material, or being distracted while you study will mean that you're not well prepared for the test. This may lead to cramming the night before, which will cause you to be physically and mentally exhausted for the test. Poor time management also contributes to feelings of stress, fear, and hopelessness as you realize you are not well prepared but don't know what to do about it.

Other times, test anxiety is not related to your preparation for the test but comes from unresolved fear. This may be a past failure on a test, or poor performance on tests in general. It may come from comparing yourself to others who seem to be performing better or from the stress of living up to expectations. Anxiety may be driven by fears of the future—how failure on this test would affect your educational and career goals. These fears are often completely irrational, but they can still negatively impact your test performance.

Elements of Test Anxiety

As mentioned earlier, test anxiety is considered to be an emotional state, but it has physical and mental components as well. Sometimes you may not even realize that you are suffering from test anxiety until you notice the physical symptoms. These can include trembling hands, rapid heartbeat, sweating, nausea, and tense muscles. Extreme anxiety may lead to fainting or vomiting. Obviously, any of these symptoms can have a negative impact on testing. It is important to recognize them as soon as they begin to occur so that you can address the problem before it damages your performance.

The mental components of test anxiety include trouble focusing and inability to remember learned information. During a test, your mind is on high alert, which can help you recall information and stay focused for an extended period of time. However, anxiety interferes with your mind's natural processes, causing you to blank out, even on the questions you know well. The strain of testing during anxiety makes it difficult to stay focused, especially on a test that may take several hours. Extreme anxiety can take a huge mental toll, making it difficult not only to recall test information but even to understand the test questions or pull your thoughts together.

Copyright © Mometrix Media. You have been licensed one copy of this document for personal use only. Any other reproduction or redistribution is strictly prohibited. All rights reserved.
This content is provided for test preparation purposes only and does not imply an endorsement by Mometrix of any particular political, scientific, or religious point of view.

Effects of Test Anxiety

Test anxiety is like a disease—if left untreated, it will get progressively worse. Anxiety leads to poor performance, and this reinforces the feelings of fear and failure, which in turn lead to poor performances on subsequent tests. It can grow from a mild nervousness to a crippling condition. If allowed to progress, test anxiety can have a big impact on your schooling, and consequently on your future.

Test anxiety can spread to other parts of your life. Anxiety on tests can become anxiety in any stressful situation, and blanking on a test can turn into panicking in a job situation. But fortunately, you don't have to let anxiety rule your testing and determine your grades. There are a number of relatively simple steps you can take to move past anxiety and function normally on a test and in the rest of life.

Physical Steps for Beating Test Anxiety

While test anxiety is a serious problem, the good news is that it can be overcome. It doesn't have to control your ability to think and remember information. While it may take time, you can begin taking steps today to beat anxiety.

Just as your first hint that you may be struggling with anxiety comes from the physical symptoms, the first step to treating it is also physical. Rest is crucial for having a clear, strong mind. If you are tired, it is much easier to give in to anxiety. But if you establish good sleep habits, your body and mind will be ready to perform optimally, without the strain of exhaustion. Additionally, sleeping well helps you to retain information better, so you're more likely to recall the answers when you see the test questions.

Getting good sleep means more than going to bed on time. It's important to allow your brain time to relax. Take study breaks from time to time so it doesn't get overworked, and don't study right before bed. Take time to rest your mind before trying to rest your body, or you may find it difficult to fall asleep.

Along with sleep, other aspects of physical health are important in preparing for a test. Good nutrition is vital for good brain function. Sugary foods and drinks may give a burst of energy but this burst is followed by a crash, both physically and emotionally. Instead, fuel your body with protein and vitamin-rich foods.

Also, drink plenty of water. Dehydration can lead to headaches and exhaustion, especially if your brain is already under stress from the rigors of the test. Particularly if your test is a long one, drink water during the breaks. And if possible, take an energy-boosting snack to eat between sections.

Along with sleep and diet, a third important part of physical health is exercise. Maintaining a steady workout schedule is helpful, but even taking 5-minute study breaks to walk can help get your blood pumping faster and clear your head. Exercise also releases endorphins, which contribute to a positive feeling and can help combat test anxiety.

When you nurture your physical health, you are also contributing to your mental health. If your body is healthy, your mind is much more likely to be healthy as well. So take time to rest, nourish your body with healthy food and water, and get moving as much as possible. Taking these physical steps will make you stronger and more able to take the mental steps necessary to overcome test anxiety.

Copyright © Mometrix Media. You have been licensed one copy of this document for personal use only. Any other reproduction or redistribution is strictly prohibited. All rights reserved.
This content is provided for test preparation purposes only and does not imply an endorsement by Mometrix of any particular political, scientific, or religious point of view.

Mental Steps for Beating Test Anxiety

Working on the mental side of test anxiety can be more challenging, but as with the physical side, there are clear steps you can take to overcome it. As mentioned earlier, test anxiety often stems from lack of preparation, so the obvious solution is to prepare for the test. Effective studying may be the most important weapon you have for beating test anxiety, but you can and should employ several other mental tools to combat fear.

First, boost your confidence by reminding yourself of past success—tests or projects that you aced. If you're putting as much effort into preparing for this test as you did for those, there's no reason you should expect to fail here. Work hard to prepare; then trust your preparation.

Second, surround yourself with encouraging people. It can be helpful to find a study group, but be sure that the people you're around will encourage a positive attitude. If you spend time with others who are anxious or cynical, this will only contribute to your own anxiety. Look for others who are motivated to study hard from a desire to succeed, not from a fear of failure.

Third, reward yourself. A test is physically and mentally tiring, even without anxiety, and it can be helpful to have something to look forward to. Plan an activity following the test, regardless of the outcome, such as going to a movie or getting ice cream.

When you are taking the test, if you find yourself beginning to feel anxious, remind yourself that you know the material. Visualize successfully completing the test. Then take a few deep, relaxing breaths and return to it. Work through the questions carefully but with confidence, knowing that you are capable of succeeding.

Developing a healthy mental approach to test taking will also aid in other areas of life. Test anxiety affects more than just the actual test—it can be damaging to your mental health and even contribute to depression. It's important to beat test anxiety before it becomes a problem for more than testing.

Study Strategy

Being prepared for the test is necessary to combat anxiety, but what does being prepared look like? You may study for hours on end and still not feel prepared. What you need is a strategy for test prep. The next few pages outline our recommended steps to help you plan out and conquer the challenge of preparation.

Step 1: Scope Out the Test

Learn everything you can about the format (multiple choice, essay, etc.) and what will be on the test. Gather any study materials, course outlines, or sample exams that may be available. Not only will this help you to prepare, but knowing what to expect can help to alleviate test anxiety.

Step 2: Map Out the Material

Look through the textbook or study guide and make note of how many chapters or sections it has. Then divide these over the time you have. For example, if a book has 15 chapters and you have five days to study, you need to cover three chapters each day. Even better, if you have the time, leave an extra day at the end for overall review after you have gone through the material in depth.

If time is limited, you may need to prioritize the material. Look through it and make note of which sections you think you already have a good grasp on, and which need review. While you are studying, skim quickly through the familiar sections and take more time on the challenging parts.

Copyright © Mometrix Media. You have been licensed one copy of this document for personal use only. Any other reproduction or redistribution is strictly prohibited. All rights reserved.
This content is provided for test preparation purposes only and does not imply an endorsement by Mometrix of any particular political, scientific, or religious point of view.

Write out your plan so you don't get lost as you go. Having a written plan also helps you feel more in control of the study, so anxiety is less likely to arise from feeling overwhelmed at the amount to cover.

Step 3: Gather Your Tools

Decide what study method works best for you. Do you prefer to highlight in the book as you study and then go back over the highlighted portions? Or do you type out notes of the important information? Or is it helpful to make flashcards that you can carry with you? Assemble the pens, index cards, highlighters, post-it notes, and any other materials you may need so you won't be distracted by getting up to find things while you study.

If you're having a hard time retaining the information or organizing your notes, experiment with different methods. For example, try color-coding by subject with colored pens, highlighters, or post-it notes. If you learn better by hearing, try recording yourself reading your notes so you can listen while in the car, working out, or simply sitting at your desk. Ask a friend to quiz you from your flashcards, or try teaching someone the material to solidify it in your mind.

Step 4: Create Your Environment

It's important to avoid distractions while you study. This includes both the obvious distractions like visitors and the subtle distractions like an uncomfortable chair (or a too-comfortable couch that makes you want to fall asleep). Set up the best study environment possible: good lighting and a comfortable work area. If background music helps you focus, you may want to turn it on, but otherwise keep the room quiet. If you are using a computer to take notes, be sure you don't have any other windows open, especially applications like social media, games, or anything else that could distract you. Silence your phone and turn off notifications. Be sure to keep water close by so you stay hydrated while you study (but avoid unhealthy drinks and snacks).

Also, take into account the best time of day to study. Are you freshest first thing in the morning? Try to set aside some time then to work through the material. Is your mind clearer in the afternoon or evening? Schedule your study session then. Another method is to study at the same time of day that you will take the test, so that your brain gets used to working on the material at that time and will be ready to focus at test time.

Step 5: Study!

Once you have done all the study preparation, it's time to settle into the actual studying. Sit down, take a few moments to settle your mind so you can focus, and begin to follow your study plan. Don't give in to distractions or let yourself procrastinate. This is your time to prepare so you'll be ready to fearlessly approach the test. Make the most of the time and stay focused.

Of course, you don't want to burn out. If you study too long you may find that you're not retaining the information very well. Take regular study breaks. For example, taking five minutes out of every hour to walk briskly, breathing deeply and swinging your arms, can help your mind stay fresh.

As you get to the end of each chapter or section, it's a good idea to do a quick review. Remind yourself of what you learned and work on any difficult parts. When you feel that you've mastered the material, move on to the next part. At the end of your study session, briefly skim through your notes again.

But while review is helpful, cramming last minute is NOT. If at all possible, work ahead so that you won't need to fit all your study into the last day. Cramming overloads your brain with more information than it can process and retain, and your tired mind may struggle to recall even

Copyright © Mometrix Media. You have been licensed one copy of this document for personal use only. Any other reproduction or redistribution is strictly prohibited. All rights reserved.
This content is provided for test preparation purposes only and does not imply an endorsement by Mometrix of any particular political, scientific, or religious point of view.

previously learned information when it is overwhelmed with last-minute study. Also, the urgent nature of cramming and the stress placed on your brain contribute to anxiety. You'll be more likely to go to the test feeling unprepared and having trouble thinking clearly.

So don't cram, and don't stay up late before the test, even just to review your notes at a leisurely pace. Your brain needs rest more than it needs to go over the information again. In fact, plan to finish your studies by noon or early afternoon the day before the test. Give your brain the rest of the day to relax or focus on other things, and get a good night's sleep. Then you will be fresh for the test and better able to recall what you've studied.

Step 6: Take a Practice Test

Many courses offer sample tests, either online or in the study materials. This is an excellent resource to check whether you have mastered the material, as well as to prepare for the test format and environment.

Check the test format ahead of time: the number of questions, the type (multiple choice, free response, etc.), and the time limit. Then create a plan for working through them. For example, if you have 30 minutes to take a 60-question test, your limit is 30 seconds per question. Spend less time on the questions you know well so that you can take more time on the difficult ones.

If you have time to take several practice tests, take the first one open book, with no time limit. Work through the questions at your own pace and make sure you fully understand them. Gradually work up to taking a test under test conditions: sit at a desk with all study materials put away and set a timer. Pace yourself to make sure you finish the test with time to spare and go back to check your answers if you have time.

After each test, check your answers. On the questions you missed, be sure you understand why you missed them. Did you misread the question (tests can use tricky wording)? Did you forget the information? Or was it something you hadn't learned? Go back and study any shaky areas that the practice tests reveal.

Taking these tests not only helps with your grade, but also aids in combating test anxiety. If you're already used to the test conditions, you're less likely to worry about it, and working through tests until you're scoring well gives you a confidence boost. Go through the practice tests until you feel comfortable, and then you can go into the test knowing that you're ready for it.

Test Tips

On test day, you should be confident, knowing that you've prepared well and are ready to answer the questions. But aside from preparation, there are several test day strategies you can employ to maximize your performance.

First, as stated before, get a good night's sleep the night before the test (and for several nights before that, if possible). Go into the test with a fresh, alert mind rather than staying up late to study.

Try not to change too much about your normal routine on the day of the test. It's important to eat a nutritious breakfast, but if you normally don't eat breakfast at all, consider eating just a protein bar. If you're a coffee drinker, go ahead and have your normal coffee. Just make sure you time it so that the caffeine doesn't wear off right in the middle of your test. Avoid sugary beverages, and drink enough water to stay hydrated but not so much that you need a restroom break 10 minutes into the

Copyright © Mometrix Media. You have been licensed one copy of this document for personal use only. Any other reproduction or redistribution is strictly prohibited. All rights reserved.
This content is provided for test preparation purposes only and does not imply an endorsement by Mometrix of any particular political, scientific, or religious point of view.

test. If your test isn't first thing in the morning, consider going for a walk or doing a light workout before the test to get your blood flowing.

Allow yourself enough time to get ready, and leave for the test with plenty of time to spare so you won't have the anxiety of scrambling to arrive in time. Another reason to be early is to select a good seat. It's helpful to sit away from doors and windows, which can be distracting. Find a good seat, get out your supplies, and settle your mind before the test begins.

When the test begins, start by going over the instructions carefully, even if you already know what to expect. Make sure you avoid any careless mistakes by following the directions.

Then begin working through the questions, pacing yourself as you've practiced. If you're not sure on an answer, don't spend too much time on it, and don't let it shake your confidence. Either skip it and come back later, or eliminate as many wrong answers as possible and guess among the remaining ones. Don't dwell on these questions as you continue—put them out of your mind and focus on what lies ahead.

Be sure to read all of the answer choices, even if you're sure the first one is the right answer. Sometimes you'll find a better one if you keep reading. But don't second-guess yourself if you do immediately know the answer. Your gut instinct is usually right. Don't let test anxiety rob you of the information you know.

If you have time at the end of the test (and if the test format allows), go back and review your answers. Be cautious about changing any, since your first instinct tends to be correct, but make sure you didn't misread any of the questions or accidentally mark the wrong answer choice. Look over any you skipped and make an educated guess.

At the end, leave the test feeling confident. You've done your best, so don't waste time worrying about your performance or wishing you could change anything. Instead, celebrate the successful completion of this test. And finally, use this test to learn how to deal with anxiety even better next time.

Review Video: Test Anxiety
Visit mometrix.com/academy and enter code: 100340

Important Qualification

Not all anxiety is created equal. If your test anxiety is causing major issues in your life beyond the classroom or testing center, or if you are experiencing troubling physical symptoms related to your anxiety, it may be a sign of a serious physiological or psychological condition. If this sounds like your situation, we strongly encourage you to seek professional help.

Copyright © Mometrix Media. You have been licensed one copy of this document for personal use only. Any other reproduction or redistribution is strictly prohibited. All rights reserved.
This content is provided for test preparation purposes only and does not imply an endorsement by Mometrix of any particular political, scientific, or religious point of view.

Online Resources

Due to our efforts to try to keep this book to a manageable length, we've created a link that will give you access to all of your online resources:

mometrix.com/resources719/texeseddiag253

It's Your Moment, Let's Celebrate It!

Share your story @mometrixtestpreparation

Copyright © Mometrix Media. You have been licensed one copy of this document for personal use only. Any other reproduction or redistribution is strictly prohibited. All rights reserved.
This content is provided for test preparation purposes only and does not imply an endorsement by Mometrix of any particular political, scientific, or religious point of view.